THE WAY

THE WAY

LIVE YOUR DREAM,
IT'S NOT A SECRET!

COSTANTINO DELLI

COS
International

The way will transform your life and the world.

DEDICATION

I dedicate this book to the silent and powerful voice that lives inside us all. I know who you are. My wish is that each of you connects to that same inner voice; it is your **C**reative **O**ptimum **S**elf. When you are connected and live from your COS, you can achieve anything including a better world for everyone.

CONTENTS

Acknowledgments   *i*

Foreword   *iii*

Introduction   *1*

Part I: Transformation

Chapter One   Transformation Is Everywhere   14
Chapter Two   Peel Away Layers   17
Chapter Three The Way with your COS   22

Part II: Transform Your Life

Chapter Four   Inspiration for *Inner* Steps   29
Chapter Five   Execute The *Inner* Steps   36

    Step 1: Journaling   37
    Step 2: Meditation   45
    Step 3: Inspirational Reading   52
    Step 4: Nature and Solitude   56
    Step 5: Well Being   61

Part III: Transform Your World

Chapter Six   Inspiration for *Outer* Steps   75
Chapter Seven   Execute The *Outer* Steps   78

    Step 6: Live with No Loose Ends   79
    Step 7: Nurture all Relationships   84
    Step 8: Be Warm and Gracious   99
    Step 9: Be Passionate and Grateful   106
    Step 10: Live from Your COS - Eyes and   113
        Ears of the Universe

Conclusion   Transforming The World –   123
        Never Ending Journey

About the Author   127

ACKNOWLEDGMENTS

My warmest gratitude goes out to all my family, friends, clients, authors, poets, actors, film makers, every day people that I know and all the people that I have met whose names I did not know. Thank you for your inspiration. It is because of these experiences that this book has emerged.

To all of you who have found The Way and are already living from your creative optimum self, thank you for your continued inspiration.

To my "home" - New York City for all the experiences and inspiration over the years and to sunny Southern California for reminding me of my birth place and inspiring me to complete this book.

Special thanks to Adrian, Leonard, Edward, Diane for your dedication and support for this book.

Christine, thank you for your friendship. Even though you are no longer here, I can still hear and miss your laughter.

My mom, thank you for the guidance and unconditional love over the years. Your strength and courage is an inspiration to all. Forza Luce!

Tanya, thank you for always challenging and supporting me to complete this book. You are one in a trillion and I love you.

And special gratitude to Bianco, the wise Pekingese, who taught me how to live in the moment and Merlin, our adopted, Blue Russian kitten - you are a teacher of life and a great typist!

FOREWORD

Every so often there comes along a person, event or book that changes people's lives; one of those people was born in Taranto, Italy and then moved with his family to the United States eight years later.

Costantino was always a "unique" child; never afraid to stand up for what is right and the constant performer. Both his parents were very hard workers leaving Cos, a nickname adopted later in life, to entertain himself most of the time through his imagination – he could create an entire game of soccer from a brick wall and his ball but what he saw was a field with twenty-two players and the stands full of screaming fans.

He always found a solution, a way to make things better. Perfect example of this, Cos' first "job" was delivering espresso in his native Italy; remember he is only five years old. He noticed that when the customer received it, the espresso was not as foamy or hot as it should be. Not one of the clients complained; however, just in their reaction and through his own observations, Cos knew this was not perfect or optimal. What did he do? Well, next delivery he covered the espresso with a saucer and presto! A very satisfied customer.

Why did I share such a simple story with you? This is a perfect example of how Costantino sees the world – he only wants the best from himself and all of us and he recognizes an opportunity or potential for greatness in even the smallest of circumstances. It could be as simple as espresso or complex as a multi billion dollar initiative, he approaches every instance the same and achieves results through efficient and quality execution.

Without efficiency and quality action in our lives, the world appears confused and clutter with stuff or "loose ends" which makes every day living a chore. Costantino has "The Way" to eliminate the clutter and live your creative optimum self. Through a simple, ten step process you can also live from your greatest self. I know this because I am living proof.

I was at a point where I felt happy, successful and enjoying life to the fullest. At this time, I began to share with a unique and selfless individual who made me realize that I did not know myself as well as I thought. He saw a "light" in me, a potential that I never knew existed. Costantino is passionate in spreading this wisdom so that organizations, businesses and individuals can also tap into their own potential. His energy and enthusiasm is genuine and very contagious!

I have seen him create "magic" through truth and wisdom, something we all have the ability to do. He is tenacious in working towards creating a better world for all by sharing his journey, successes, disappointments and unending curiosity to learn more from everyone he encounters.

Since this time, I have, and still am, connecting with my greatest self. I have tapped into my creativity and can see the dramatic changes in my life, personally and professionally. I follow "The Way" and share my own success stories as I know they inspire others to do the same.

The pages before you will not only transform your life but those around you; embrace them, live them, love them; you won't be sorry!

So now you are at that point in your life; a book has come along that will change your life. It certainly has changed mine. I am proud to say that Costantino Delli is now my husband and I share his passion and continue on this journey with him.

Tanya Perrin

INTRODUCTION

This book will guide you to live your greatest life. I am inspired to write it after years of debate with friends and clients whether people would be interested in reading The Way. I have dedicated my entire life in personal transformation, and through my consulting practice guiding businesses, organizations and communities to transform or improve. Like many of you, I have lived an exciting, ever changing life, full of ups and downs and above all, passion. What I am most passionate about is transformation, all forms, from nature, personal, business and community. I feel exhilarated after observing an individual, our environment or a being transform or improve to something greater. There is great beauty in this observation and it brings me an abundance of joy. I thought I was satisfied continuing on this path through my business using the steps outlined in this book. But in the last six months, I have been hearing the universe, through all its forms, speak to me that I need to write and share The Way with all of you. Each day friends, clients and strangers share with me that we live in a world of injustice, suffering, anger and disappointment. While this may be true on the surface, many people know of a better way to live.

The final push that I needed it to complete this book was when I attended an International Forum, chaired by Deepak Chopra. The forum was held to connect leaders from various organizations, businesses and individuals and share the contributions they are making to bring unity and transformation in the world. During the session, Deepak asked each of us to complete what he called a "soul profile". This profile consisted of several questions about who we are, our passions and what contributions we wish to make to the world. He suggested that as we share who we are on the inside, we can learn more about each other and see if we can make a connection, support and leverage our work. I connected with the questions and realized that I needed to share The Way with the rest of you. I realized that life would not allow me to move forward until I completed this.

The Way is comprised of steps divided into parts that I call *inner* and *outer*. The *outer* steps are based on five principles that I have successfully used in my professional career. These principles are customized as needed, serving the client to execute a strategy to advance and transform their business. For example, building solid relationships across all business units, leverage what works and implement processes that are most efficient and encourage creative thinking. These principles when properly aligned and executed bring about changes, improvements and transformation. The key to the success is always in the proper execution, not only in business but, as you will see, also in personal transformation.

Every day I am reminded by my personal clients, friends and every day people how difficult it is to execute or follow through with something. People know what they need to do; eat less or exercise to lose weight, stop the excessive drinking, get out of a toxic relationship or get a better job. But for various reasons, they are not able to get started or stay on a constant path. Even the many books that are in the market today, are full of knowledge and experience, but not many give a simple, organized guide that inspire and empower people to execute and remain constant. By tapping into the business success stories that I and my clients have experienced, I will share with you the five *outer* steps that will bring success to you in all aspects of your life and guide you to your creative optimum self or COS.

The *inner* steps discussed are based on my personal experiences, science and the arts. These steps have always been part of my life, even though at times I may have neglected a few of the steps. For instance, as a child I always enjoyed sharing time with nature and in solitude but never felt lonely. As I began reading and writing poetry in my 20's, I knew that through nature and silence I was tapping into an inner source for inspiration. Then in 1996, when I began studying professional acting in New York City and reading classic books, Constantin Stanislavski's "An Actor Prepares", I realized the connection between overall well being to inspiration. Acting and poetry teaches that your body is a vessel or an instrument and if you treat it well, you will tap into an unlimited source of inspiration. For most people, this is the most challenging aspect of transformation to connect with this source, but once you have it you can then live from this place each moment of your life and your life will change forever. I will guide you through the *inner* steps and over time as you practice, you will live from your creative optimum self, and as you incorporate both the *inner* and *outer* steps, you will inspire others to tap into their COS and transform as well. By following The Way together, we can make our world a better place.

I Guarantee it!

I guarantee that if you incorporate the *inner* and *outer* steps outlined in this book into your daily life, your life will improve, in a measurable way. Most people see the results after a couple of months, others might take more time. Many people find the *inner* steps most challenging because they may not be familiar with this process or it takes time to peel away the layers they have accumulated over time. Sometimes, the steps need to be customized based on individual circumstances. My guarantee is this: Read this book, complete all the exercises and incorporate the *inner* and *outer* steps into your daily life, and you will see an improvement in your life. If after ninety days, you are not able to measure an improvement in your life, please send me a note at cos@cosinternational.org with your specific situation and we will schedule a complimentary session to discuss how you can reconnect with your COS.

Before we begin this journey, there are two things we need to do. Sign a contract and complete a self assessment. We need to do an assessment of your current state, this way you will be able to measure and track your progress at any time during this journey.

Contract

I know that it is very easy for all of us to say that we will do something and then for various reasons, sometimes we do not execute with our plan. But I also know that writing is powerful and when we put it in writing, it takes a deeper meaning. It becomes a contract – it stares right in front of our face and it reminds us of the promised we made to ourselves.

You may find this silly, but I urge you to have this agreement with yourself.

"Today is _____ and I, _____(name)_____, on my own free will, agree to be open and consider the steps and guidelines set forth in The Way.

My intention is to inspire you in a harmonious way for you to execute these steps on your own, not to force you into something you do not want to do. Give it a try, be reasonable and commit to it for a few months. If you follow the steps, creatively, I know they will guide you to a better life.

Self Assessment
Now that you have agreed to consider The Way, please answer the following questions and record the results.

1. Date and time of this assessment
2. Your body measurements: weight, height, waist/hip/chest size, body fat
3. Measure or ask your doctor to take your blood pressure
4. Determine your cholesterol level through blood work.

Answer yes or no to following questions:
5. Do you feel lethargic at times?
6. Do you get headaches or stomachaches at times?
7. Do you feel foggy at times?
8. Do you find yourself always eating or munching?
9. Do you think you enjoy your food or do you rush through it?
10. Do you feel heavy after eating a meal?

11. Do you feel sad or lonely at times?

12. Do you get angry or get upset easily at times?

13. Do you think you have a temper or are quick to judge things at times?

14. Do you worry; have fears or anxiety or experience stress at times?

15. Do you feel an emptiness inside of you?

16. What is your definition of a spirit?

17. For this question, select a or b. Do you think that
  a) you are a human being who sometimes has spiritual experiences or
  b) you are a spiritual being who is also living as a human being at this moment?

Once you have recorded this initial assessment, you can use it as a baseline as you progress on this journey and you can compare it to the next time you complete the same assessment.

Okay, you are now ready to begin this journey of transformation.

Transformation begins each new day.

PART I

TRANSFORMATION

Transformation exists everywhere. I define transformation as to bring "light" into a person, creature of life, event or situation, environment, organization and the world. This "light" can be manifested through efficiency, order, joy, peace, harmony or love, just to name a few. Many people are doing great work in various ways around the world to make this place a more loving and peaceful life for everyone. But some are not aware how their work is having a positive impact and others do not think that their help is needed. And great many people have simply given up on this world, they think the world is going up in flames; there is violence, war, terror, poverty, and disease everywhere, we get reminded of this each day. It is true that there exists many sufferings in this world, but because suffering exists today, it is not a given that it will exist tomorrow. Society has a tendency to play the victim part very easily by accepting the way things are because that is the way it is and can not be changed. Society says that we are all different from each other - we have different religions, political beliefs, cultures, we look different, we have different labels, needs and society accepts that violence, for example, rises as a result. We disagree, we argue and somebody always wins, it is just the way it is. Well, my experiences in life have taught me otherwise.

We can live a life where we celebrate our differences by showing compassion, where we learn from our mistakes through our experiences and gain wisdom by taking responsibilities for our actions. I have learned that beyond our differences, there is a common ground that we all walk on. Some people understand this but are hesitant to practice it in their lives because they are afraid to be judged by society while a few understand and live by this and are making their contribution in transforming the world. But most of the people have no clue or at this time they are simply not aware of it. By becoming aware of The Way and incorporating it into your life, you will experience a shift in your awareness. You will become more curious about life and it will push you to grow, evolve, and reconnect with your creative optimum self. From here, you can live your greatest life.

Transformation is all around us — be aware and you will see life in a whole new way.

CHAPTER ONE

TRANSFORMATION IS EVERYWHERE

Transformation is all around us, in business, in nature - from a sunrise to sunset, from rain turning to water that we drink, flowers blooming, the birth of a life - and in personal transformation - anger turning to joy, realization of a dream, reaching a goal, finding a solution, evolving into a wiser person. Recently, I have realized that I am most passionate in personal transformation because of the knowledge and wisdom that can be gained from the experience.

I was born in Taranto, Italy, a beautiful, ancient, southern city in the Apulia region. My parents owned a restaurant in the newer section of town. I loved my childhood – it was spent between playing soccer in the parking lots, on the beach, hanging out in the restaurant helping out my dad at the cash register and going to school. At age five, I had the first big change in my life. I almost died from a simple appendix operation. Imagine this, the top doctor in the city, operated on me while intoxicated and forgot to untie my intestine after he removed the appendix. Go figure! For three days, I was not well – white as a ghost in the hospital and could not eat, drink or move. According to the experts, it was all normal after such operation. If it wasn't for my mom's tenacity, I would not be writing to you today. She persisted until she got the eyes and ears of a true expert, visiting from Switzerland, to have a look at me. He said he would do what he can and asked my mom if she was a woman of great faith, which she was. So I was back on the operating table and remembered lying underneath these huge lamps and thought to myself, is this the end? Where will I go? But, somehow I knew that I would be OK, I was not afraid. The surgery was a success and after a long recovery I was happy to be home.

A few years later, my parents decided to visit family we had in America, in Trenton NJ. My mom and I visited the great "land of opportunity". I was not happy to leave home but my mom convinced me that it would be an adventure to visit a new place. But my first experience on a plane made me very nervous; it was huge, and what language were these people speaking? When we finally landed at Kennedy Airport, there was a snow blizzard, first time I experienced snow in my life. It was beautiful to look at, but the cold was too much for a Southern beach boy. It was not easy to adjust and after a few trips back and forth, my mom and dad decided to leave the beautiful and warm Taranto for the industrial capital city, Trenton. Talk about contrasts!

And the personal transformation stories keep coming as I will share with you in this book. As I said, transformation is all around us. It is part of life and if there are parts of life that are not in harmony, we can change it. But some people and society, in general, do not agree with this. Why?

Peel away layers and you will see beauty in all things.

CHAPTER TWO

PEEL AWAY LAYERS

Society has a practice of teaching us that if we follow religious or political rules and laws, we will be good citizens and if we are really good, we can go to some form of heaven. In a way, society has taken on this responsibility to take care of or control us by informing us of what we need to do to live a happy life. But our soul already knows how to live a joyous life but many people are not connected with their soul. This book is about guiding you to find your inner truth, your COS. We need to remove some of what our ancestors have taught us from religions, cultures and traditions and replace with wisdom and knowledge already contained in each of us. This wisdom and knowledge has always existed. Indeed, if you read ancient documents, poetry, essays across many philosophies and religions, you will notice a common theme. They all share experiences that are divine, miraculous, and discuss the light, harmony, peace and love. They existed then and exist today. Like the Bible written centuries ago, one can be written today filled with parables and passages from today's experiences. In a way, life has remained the same. But it is easy to forget this given the leaps and bounds we have made in technology that can be a distraction to the true nature of reality. We should use technology to enrich our lives in making things easier for us but not allow it to change the true reality of our lives.

Society has taught us that we, human beings, are not perfect. We are only human – this is the "poor me" victim speaking and we justify our weaknesses. Yes, the human body has limitations but if you allow your soul to govern your life, it will give your body what it needs to stay healthy and alive so that it can be the channel for your soul. If you live from the soul today, you can create the life you wish to live. How can you begin to live from your soul? You begin by removing the "layers", past beliefs and false notions that have become part of every day life.

As you remove the layers and peel away years of disappointments, angers, fears and anxieties you will find your soul inside. This soul is a beautiful, safe and a guide that will enrich your life. The soul will speak to you through your inner self and through others – friends and strangers. The same soul lives everywhere and it is only natural to hear the universe speak to you. You just need to be present, alert and from the soul to hear it. You need to be "clean" from the past. This is difficult for many because we pile up stuff in our heads and stay connected to them. But there is a way. When you execute the *inner* steps, beginning with journaling as discussed later, you will have more clarity in your mind and live more in the present. Here, you will have more control of your life and design the kind of life you wish to live. But first, we need to stop playing the victim and take control.

We have been raised in a world that nourishes and supports the victim behavior of people. And as a result, this creates layers, inefficiencies and blocks us from living the life we were born to live. A victim is much more than the "poor me" tendency, there is another form that exists that creates stress in our lives. Many people have a tendency to just accept that they are not passionate and can not excel at something because they are not born with great skills or talent and they are not worthy of things - they are just lazy. These people play a game with life and choose to live a certain life; they say to themselves that they are not capable of being happy, optimal or a light. They choose to act in a certain, negative way, and society nourishes this by supporting their behavior. Hence, you have those who have addictions like alcohol and drugs and these actions are supported – "poor guy, he is this way because of his addiction". Instead, they should be guided to realize that what they are doing is causing pain and suffering to themselves and the world at large. They should be guided to take action and make a change for the better.

We are citizens of the world, and as citizens, we have a responsibility to be the eyes and ears of the universe. That is, we need to be protectors of the universe. How can we do this you say? By living a way of life that creates harmony and love in the world and not enabling the victims. Please do not confuse this with supporting and nourishing people who need assistance and ask for help. It is our responsibility to help these people, but those who just complain about things and do nothing about it; we need to do more. We need to remind them that they are playing the victim; we are not responsible for their issues and that the same inner wisdom that lives in us lives in them. They are capable to achieve happiness if they take the appropriate steps. If we all encourage and support this way, we will empower them to take control of their lives and transform.

Transformation can take place when we are aware; at times this is not easy. I have been a victim myself in my life and I see many people behave this way; the key is to recognize this so that you can make changes. This awareness will guide you to transform your life from the victim to the wise. And living with wisdom and knowledge is the only way to live.

The Way with your COS is like scuba diving - the deeper you go, the more beautiful the pearl.

CHAPTER THREE

THE WAY WITH YOUR COS

What is The Way? Throughout ancient times, The Way or Tao is described as a way to live that is aligned with the universe. The Way is how to live a life of peace, love and pure bliss. Your COS is the Way. It is the way that gives you what you need to live an optimum and creative life. It is easy to be happy when everything goes well, but how can you be happy all the times – during disappointments, failures, and losses in your lives? How can this be possible?

Many people think that it is not realistic that this world can adopt a utopia even after so many wonderful leaders, poets and religious figures have tried the same before. The fact that these inspirational people have lived in the past is proof that this is possible. They have advanced our civilization through their books, teachings and actions. Books can be inspirational but the key is in the execution. In my business and personal experiences this is the biggest challenge for individuals - to follow through on great ideas. I have dedicated my entire life in guiding others to learn the art of execution.

My intention for this book is to inspire and empower you to execute the COS *inner* and *outer* steps and observe how you can transform to your greatest self while transforming the world around you.

The COS steps are based on the knowledge that we are spiritual beings who live in physical bodies for this moment. This spiritual being or soul that lives in you always needs to express itself but if your physical body, or ego, is absorbed by societal layers it gets in the way and the soul can not live. If it does not live, then you lose your true self. Thus, it becomes very important to keep the layers away by removing all negativity from your lives - toxic people, situations, and environment. When we do this, we achieve peace and tranquility and can hear the soul again. Once we hear the soul, we see ourselves connected to the universal flow, the creator of all good things. This voice is who we are, we are all one and belong to the same source. We have different physical identities, but the soul is the same. If we can all live from the soul, then we will achieve harmony and unity. This is The Way… your creative optimum self.

Once the basic principles of these COS steps are embraced and practiced daily, then not only will you transform your life, you will inspire others to do the same. Upon executing the steps, you will enjoy greater health in all areas of your life - body, mind, spirit, careers, relationships and financials. Are you ready to transform your life? These steps are simple and practical, they are not based on any religion or political beliefs. You do not need any special skills or education to practice them. As you incorporate them into your daily life, just like you breathe air every day, you will connect with the inner guide and over time you will transform. We all have choices and the choice we make today determines the life we will have tomorrow. And if we want to have a better world tomorrow, we need to start today, wherever we are and whatever we are doing.

The first five steps, *inner*, focus on you. Some people may find this challenging as they are not accustomed in putting attention on themselves – they were not raised this way, or they are afraid to address their fears, or think that it is a selfish act to think of oneself. But only when you truly know yourself, and you live from your soul, can you help others. Incorporate these simple, practical steps into your daily life and you will see yourself in a new wonderful way.

The last five steps, *outer*, focus on how you interact with the rest of the world. If you practice the *inner* steps daily, you will naturally evolve into the *outer* steps and you will inspire others to do the same. You will be living proof that the world can indeed be governed by peace, love and harmony. Be open and complete all the exercises that follow the steps and allow your imagination to guide you into this wonderful journey.

Transforming your life is a journey worth taking.

PART II

TRANSFORM YOUR LIFE

Now that you are ready to transform your life, I will share with you the five *inner* steps that will guide you to connect with your creative optimum self; journaling, meditation, inspirational reading, nature and solitude, and well being. I recommend that you go through the steps in order the first time, and then you can revisit specific ones in more detail.

Everyone who has gone through this process has gained much wisdom and knowledge from these steps and many revisit them often at different stages of their journey. Please pace yourself and don't rush through it. Be kind to yourself.

Inner steps are ancient wisdom for the personal and universal soul.

CHAPTER FOUR

INSPIRATION FOR *INNER* STEPS

The *inner* steps are based on my personal life experiences, the arts and science. Journaling is the first step. I began keeping a journal at a very young age in my life. I was six years old, in Italy and in first grade. Our teacher introduced us in recording a daily chronicle into our notebooks - our homework each night was to write about our day. I was very loyal in writing in my notebook and kept it as my family moved from Italy to the United States in 1974. For the next four years, we resided in six different residences until we finally purchased a home. During the move, I lost my notebooks which made me very sad because they meant a great deal to me. I stopped writing on a regular basis and would only write when I experienced a crisis in my life, like my father's passing or when I reached a low point in my life in 1995.

Then in 2002, I decided to start a new journal and record all the major events in my life from birth. Today, I regularly write in my journal, it is now reached about 500 pages and counting. The primary reason that I write into my journal daily is that it keeps me grounded. I learn a great deal about myself by writing how I feel on a particular day or the impact experiences are having in my life. As I write in my journal, I find solutions to problems, it guides me on how to interact with other people and deal with situations and provides me with insight and wisdom about life in general. It also allows my creative side to awaken, thus the emergence of the following poems written in 1997:

live in the moment
in the moment, a circle of light will shine from above.
This light, will keep you focused and light up your surrounding, so that you can see.
When you can see, you are in the moment. The present.
When you are in the present, you are the light.
the light is within you.

The beauty of nature that i see
with my eyes,
is still present within when
my eyes are shut.

I know where i am but i could be anywhere,
i see the images of life before me
and i know my eyes are closed,
i feel the breeze of spring days sweep by me
and i know that today is fall,
i touch the thin air that fills the sky,
still i can see nature from up above.

I know why i come here even
> when i do not recognize this place.
I sit by the waters and wait for life to come to me.
i hear the wind passing through me
> leaving me with the seeds of life's secrets,
i taste the sweet juices of the seeds as
> they travel deep in my soul,
i feel the unfertilized beings from the womb of creation
> and cradle them in my lips,
i plant the seeds of my future
> in the eternal place of timeless awareness.

I see the beautiful seeds resting in silence close to me.
i see my unbound destiny unravel from the resting seed.

As the light turns to darkness,
i awaken, and i find myself resting above.

I know i have been here before but
> i don't know when.

As i sit under an oak tree by the lake,
i observe nature expressing its beauty,

i see the sun warming the still water,
i feel the breeze sweeping the flowers with ecstasy,
i hear the birds singing and dancing freely,
i touch the source of all creation, love.
I know now that i come here often.

It is silent, it is peaceful, it is still.
It is a place of haven, it is my place,
and i can always find it in my heart.

Writing is also part of the life of a professional actor. Like many actors, I began performing at the young age of five for my family and friends. Then as an adult, I studied professionally and learned a great deal about the link between the acting process and life. What I truly love and appreciate about acting is the overall process of bringing a character to life. And part of the process is to do research, study and write about the character. You learn a great deal about the character by writing out the likes and dislikes - what he likes to wear, what his fears are and his dreams. Over time an actor will create the psyche of the character and will use this outline to shape his performance. And this is the connection to journaling - writing becomes a useful tool for an actor to prepare for a performance. Journaling is the first *inner* step; it is the starting point for change.

Meditation is the second *inner* step. I was raised Roman Catholic and prayer was part of my daily routine. I prayed like the church taught us and what I remember most about praying as a child was that it always brought me peace afterwards. Over the years, prayer has evolved into a form of meditation that I practice now which is very different from the early days. Still, the outcome of my meditation is peace. I use meditation to tap into my silence and source of inspiration and what emerges is a beautiful piece of life that fuels my day. You can also have this source of inspiration with meditation and I will show you how.

The third *inner* step is inspirational reading. My soul is awakened and inspired by reading material that stir up emotions, stimulate my inner senses and intellect. It takes me away from my daily routine and brings me back fresh and ready to deal with life. This third *inner* step will bring you closer to reach your COS.

Nature and solitude is the fourth *inner* step. Ever since I was a child, I always enjoyed spending time with nature. I grew up very close to the beach and it became my favorite past time, to swim, play and build sand castles. I always felt safe and protected, not only during the day, also at night walking under the stars. My parents would take us every night for a walk along the beautiful beachfront promenade in Taranto. I remembered walking and holding my father's hand and looking up to the stars and counting them in an imaginary square I created in the sky. I would usually fall asleep and my father had to carry me home but I always felt refreshed. And today, spending time with nature remains a big part of my life. Even a short walk through the park or by a lake, can be a welcomed time out during a busy day. The same is true for spending time alone, whether or not this is with nature. I love sharing time with all kinds of people but at times I do enjoy spending time with my own thoughts. As a poet or actor, this is also the case. I write my best work if I am alone watching a sunset or looking at a river, the sea or the mountains. Even in solitude you can still feel a connection with friends, family and every one else.

Overall well being is the fifth and final *inner* step. When I was a child, my eating habits were determined more by my parents, the Italian culture and their traditions. Over the years, I learned to listen to my body more on how to take better care of my body by choosing foods that make my body comfortable. Not only is what you eat important but exercise as well, which has always been a part of my life. I grew up playing soccer until I reached my 30's and today I enjoy swimming, biking, hiking and running on the beach. I can feel all the benefits that my body receives by staying fit and exercising regularly. Keeping the body in excellent form is very important if I am writing poetry or this book. My creativity is fueled while exercising and was a great support while writing this book.

And there you have it – this is how the five *inner* steps have emerged. You can execute these steps into your own life and create the life you want…let's get started.

Executing the inner steps will make your dreams come true.

CHAPTER FIVE

EXECUTE THE *INNER* STEPS

Now that you have the source of inspiration for the *inner* steps, let me show you how you can incorporate these steps into your daily life. Each step concludes with a written or visual exercise. I recommend that you complete each exercise the first time through and revisit them at a later time to observe and compare changes with the results.

Journaling is like having a best friend with you - it inspires and nourishes your soul.

STEP 1: **JOURNALING**

Journaling is an amazing tool that will guide you on this journey today and for years to come. Keeping a journal allows you to safely express the inner voices, desires, and thoughts that emerge during good and not so good times; it peels away layers around the core essence of one's soul. Because of social conditioning, lack of awareness and difficult experiences, people accumulate fears, worries, anxieties and other toxic emotions. These energies form layers around the true self and control the way you live your life. If you are not aware of it, your actions will be fueled by these negative and toxic layers. And as a result you will be unhappy. If you continue living this way, you will turn into a victim and base your entire life on the "poor me" syndrome. You will feel powerless, unworthy, inferior and depressed. This can be transformed, and it all begins with journaling.

Here's how to begin journaling. Find a quiet time and place where you can bring a notebook to be with your thoughts. If you can be with nature or have a harmonious view would help, but you can do this anywhere. Open the notebook and write whatever thoughts, ideas, and voices you are experiencing at the moment. For those who have never kept some kind of journal in their lives, it may be difficult to begin writing. But I assure you, that once you begin, it will empower you to change your life. Write everything down – what you are feeling, experiencing, thinking of. If you are worried about something, thinking of what to make for dinner, hoping that you get a call for work, anything and everything. If you are experiencing pain in your back, a phone call you need to make, happy that you shared a meal with your old friend yesterday, you love the way the trees are moving at this moment. Write everything that you are thinking, experiencing and feeling.

It will vary how much you will write based on how open you are with this process, and what is going on in your life at the time. It could take ten minutes to over an hour for each sitting. Some of my clients biggest excuse for not writing is that they do not have time in a day to write. And I usually say to them that writing will change your life - isn't that worth a few minutes of your time in a day? Even after one sitting, you will feel better. Write until you have nothing to say and you will notice a change in you. You will feel lighter, you will have a sense of relief, most people will feel peaceful, others may cry because of the events they have shared. This more peaceful state of mind is who you really are. And as you continue this process over time, you will gain more peace and awareness. You will become aware of your thoughts. Most people who have these layers are not aware that this peaceful state exists in their soul. They simply carry out the negative thoughts or layers that lives in their mind.

If one has a sense of doubt about something, all their actions are fueled by this hesitation and this expression will be picked up by others. Instead, if the layers can be removed by writing them down, forgiving yourself and heal, then you become aware that you have an inner wisdom. This inner wisdom will "talk" to you and guide your life. This is your COS. Journaling cleanses all the layers, conditioning, or self doubt that has accumulated over the years, and replaces it with awareness. This awareness is the ability to be observer of the thoughts that occupy the mind and realize that you are aware of it. You become aware of your own awareness.

Some people spend their entire life wanting to reach this state of awareness, while others achieve it during their life and a few may never achieve it. Be patient with yourself and if you practice journaling on a daily basis combined with the remaining steps, you will learn to become the observer of your thoughts. Once you become the observer, you will realize that you are not the thoughts that you have, they are the layers that have accumulated over time. By writing, you will peel away the layers and meet the real you – the silent observer who has lived, lives and will live long after your body has completed its journey in this lifetime. In this way, you have more control of your life and you can replace your thoughts with those that will bring happiness to you and create the life you desire. When you release these thoughts or intentions with clarity and non interference, they connect with the universal awareness, that we are all part of, to orchestrate the events for us. This is the mind of the universe, the one soul that connects us all. They are one of the same. And this inner wisdom provides you with the correct insights and guidance for your life.

Your COS will speak to you and give you insights or clues to why you did something, the solution to a problem, or the appropriate next step in your life. I like to share with you something I wrote about ten years ago as I began to journal again after a long absence. During one of my morning session, I began writing and this is the result:

...when I am tired, I find me in a swamp.

I pain as I try to feel air,
I pain as I try to touch the passage of time,
I pain as I try to see the light glow over the horizon,
I pain as I try to hear the stars embark on their journey
from heaven.

I pain in try 'cause I find myself in a swamp.

My limbs are locked in chains from the fatigue and sleep-
lessness of my weary nights,
I sink lower in the dark swamp, drowning, taking all the
breath of my youthful seed,
Ultimately I reach the end of the dreadful swamp and
hear a thump in my head...I find myself at the pit of my
mind.

There lies the swamp.

I hear a laugh,
I see a smile,
And I feel the warmth of a mother's womb,
My spirit is watching me from the stars of tomorrow,
Wondering the whys of my pain and
The whys of my neglect to grab the rope of tomorrow.

I saw no rope to save my poor body.
Spirit smiles and tells me to open my eyes so I could see
the moment,

I could not see where I was until I found myself hope-lessly. In the dungeon of my mind.

As spirit spreads out the wings of yesterday
To return to the bright lights of the future,
I hear a thump in my heart and a whisper as soft as silk,
I am with you, find me…

"Find me" is a phrase heard by many who have taken this journey of transformation. At some point in their lives, if they are not living from their soul, and usually during some dramatic or low point in their lives, they hear a calling from the inner wisdom to find themselves. For those who accept the invitation and do the work to become aware of who they really are, they are rewarded in finding their soul and trans-form their lives.

I would like to share a story of how journaling has guided my life. I went away on vacation alone for a few days in Antigua in January 2005. One night, I sat on the beach under the stars and wrote in my journal. I wrote about the kind of woman I wanted to meet, what she looked like and more importantly her personality, the kind of person she would be on the inside. It was pretty detailed. Later in February, on the 14th to be exact, I went to use the health club facility in my residence in New York. It was about 6 p.m. and as I worked out, here walks in a beautiful, engaging and bright woman. She comes straight to me and immediately connected with my eyes and I knew right there that she was the one I wrote about in my journal. Yes, it is true, I met Tanya on Valentine's night and we have been together ever since. She is the most fascinating person I have ever met. We can do anything together – even reading a foreign phone book together is fun. And it all started in my journal!

Writing in a journal is an amazing tool that will guide your life. It will keep you connected with your creative optimum self.

Step 1 Recap: Journaling

A recap of journaling and the steps you can take now to execute and be on your way to transform your life.

1. Set aside each morning and evening to write in your journal. This can be a notebook or electronically. Initially, I recommend a notebook and longhand. Set aside twenty minutes to begin but there may be times that you will need more time. Be flexible. Do find a quiet place where you will not be disturbed by anything or anyone. If you can sit with nature, all the better.

2. In the morning, write about how you are feeling, the dreams that you had, other thoughts or worries that creep up in your writing. Do NOT judge them. Just write and observe. You are cleansing away the layers that you have at the moment and you are seeking wisdom from your soul. The soul will speak to you and give you insight into the significance of the dream, for example, or why you are feeling a sort of way. When your writing reaches a more peaceful state, you may begin thinking about your day. You can create a to-do list of things that you need to do for the day. You can write and visualize about your day. This writing will give you the fuel to carry out the work for the day and provide you the wisdom and insight.

3. In the evening, write about your day. Do a chronicle of your day. How you felt during the day, what happened,

a moment of weakness you experienced, a difficult situation you encountered, a magical moment you experienced. Document your day as if your day is up on a movie screen and you are the observer of this movie. Observe your actions, and you will gain insight into your experiences. You may realize that you should have acted in a kinder way, or you are not happy how you handle a certain situation and you promise yourself to do it differently next time. After writing you will feel lighter and you will have a more peaceful sleep.

4. Keep your journal private. You may want to share some of what you write to someone who you are connected with at a very deep level, who you can trust and will not judge you. Even then, don't share the journal, just discuss it verbally. This allows you to protect your writing. It is your haven. Keep it safe.

5. Over a long period of time, your writing may change and become not legible because of the speed of your thoughts. This is normal as you enter a deeper state of awareness and your thoughts on paper become like waves on top of the ocean or like energy traveling at the speed of light.

Exercise

For this exercise, read the following questions and without thinking too much, quickly answer them in your journal. Write as much as you want for each question even if it takes you places not related to the question.

1. I wish I was _____. Why?
2. I love to _____. Why?

3. I hope to _____. Why?
4. One day, I will _____. How do you know?
5. I know that _____. How do you know? And why do you say that?
6. I believe in _____. Why?
7. I see beauty in _____.Why?
8. I have anxieties when _____. How do you over come them?
9. I am relaxed when _____. Why?
10. I am _____. Why?

Observe your thoughts and let your writing take you deeper into your self. Writing will trigger things that you may not have thought of. Over time, you will learn more about yourself and you will know what you need to do to improve your life.

As you practice with journaling, you will evolve into the next step - meditation.

*Meditation unleashes your imagination - you
can see, feel and hear beautiful things with
your eyes closed.*

STEP 2: **MEDITATION**

Meditation is the next step in achieving your creative
optimum self and guiding you to change your life.
There are many useful books today that discuss and teach
the various techniques of meditation. I started meditating
ten years ago and continue to do so today. At first, I did not
know when or how to do it. Over time, I realized, and my
clients confirm today, that by journaling first, it clears away
the thoughts that occupy your mind and brings the mind to a
silent place and ready to meditate.

Journaling unravels all the layers that live inside of you
so that you can begin to experience stillness during meditation. This stillness inside of you allows you to hear your
innate wisdom. After journaling, close your eyes and put your
attention on your breathing. Keep your attention there and
allow yourself to quiet the mind. This may be difficult as you
may hear rambling of thoughts or voices going through your
mind. This is normal. When I first started I heard voices like
- what am I doing sitting here, when I need to make a phone
call, or pick up groceries, or I didn't pay the bill, or I hope
Debbie calls me tonight, and dozens of other thoughts. And

I thought it was normal for me to have these thoughts. After all, we are human beings - we have a brain that we are born with and have been raised to be "thinkers". It has been said by many wise individuals, that a great form of knowledge and wisdom is the ability for someone to observe and be aware of their own thoughts. It has taken me a long time to truly understand and experience what this means, and it is quite simple, all these voices are not who you truly are. Once these voices quiet down and disappear, you will achieve inner stillness or a meditative state. This is your inner wisdom.

That is why it is useful to meditate after journaling. Journaling "cleans" out your human mind and allows you to tap into this inner silence. There you can visualize and see yourself as someone much greater than your physical self, one with the universal world, beyond the physical body. You are a spiritual being first, a precious soul whose source is the same for all creatures on this earth. Even more amazing is what scientists tell us today that we are made up of the same atoms and molecules that exist in the universe and most of this is made up of empty space. This empty space is full of possibilities.

It has taken me a long time to understand this and till this day, I am still learning more on what this actually means. But I know today and science tells us that this earth that we live in is traveling at the speed of light, yet our physical eyes can not see it. Why? Because our eyes are not made up to see this. There are things that our eyes can not see and yet they are true. I will give you a simple example.

Imagine standing on the side of a highway and watching a car ride by at 20 miles per hour. At this speed, you will probably be able to identify the make, model and color of the car and the condition of the car and even see if the driver is a man or woman. Now imagine, that the car is going by faster, say 50 miles per hour. At this speed, you may not recognize who the driver is and probably not be able to tell if the car is in good shape or not. If the speed of the car is even faster, at 100 or 150 miles per hour, you will be able to pick up less information about the car and the driver. If the car is going 200 or all the way up to 500 miles per hour, your eyes, will not able to describe the car or driver in detail because it is going too fast. It flies right by you. Now imagine a racing car that goes by 1,000 miles per hour, I don't think that there is a car today that goes this fast, but if it did, we would all agree, that we would not be able to describe the car as we stand on the highway because the car would fly right by us. Now, imagine a car or anything flying pass you at 10,000 miles per hour, you will not be able to see anything. It will be like wind blowing right by you.

When scientists speak of the speed of light, it is defined to be about 186,282 miles per second. That is right, per second. This translates to about 670,615,200 miles per hour, over 670 million miles per hour. It is huge – lighting speed and un-imaginable with our eyes. At this amazing speed, life takes on a different meaning. At this level, we can see that we, humans and other creatures of this life, are all exchanging the same atoms and molecules, the same energy. At this level, we are one.

If we live our lives from the knowledge that we are one, we live a more complete life because we have true knowledge of who we really are. And when we know who we really are, we feel safer and have knowledge that we are loved from this wonderful universe. What does this have to do with meditation? Well, if you can visualize this state as you meditate on the daily basis, it will help you to stay connected to your true self and not forget who you really are. Yes, we are human beings and we have limitations, but we are spiritual beings first and we are part of the same energy that lives in this infinite universe. It is very easy to forget this because most of us live a very hectic life and get preoccupied with daily mundane things. Meditation will keep you grounded and connected with this knowledge.

Step 2 Recap: Meditation

Meditating on a daily basis will keep you grounded and connected with your inner guide or creative optimum self. Here are guidelines on how and when to meditate:

1. Meditate daily after journaling in the morning and evening and any time during the day when you feel like you are disconnected from your true self. Set aside about ten to fifteen minutes in a quiet, comfortable place.

2. Close your eyes and focus on your breathing. As thoughts come up, let them go through you as you stay focused on your breathing. Reach a state of mind that you have no thoughts. If you are not able to achieve this, either write out these thoughts in your journal or use music and incense to create a more peaceful place.

3. As you focus on your breath with no random thoughts, imagine that you are more than this physical body. Imagine yourself connected with all around you, the air, the sky, the trees, and the rest of nature. Imagine that you are one connected with the universe, that you are a beam of light that is everywhere. See yourself as one with the world. You are safe in this world.

4. As this beam of light, imagine that you give this bright

light to where you are in the moment now. Give this wonderful light to your body, to where you are sitting and to everything and everyone around you. Shine this light to the city you live in, to all people you know and to the places you go. Bless the world all around you with your shining light.

5. Now imagine the rest of your day, places you need to go and people you need to see and things you need to do. As you imagine this, give your light, energy and focus to all this around you. You are blessing the day. Give love to your remaining day by giving your light and love. Be thankful for all that you have and see yourself giving this warm and gracious light to all creatures of the world.

6. As you slowly open your eyes, become aware of your surroundings and allow what you experienced during meditation to guide your day. Stay alert, aware and connected to your creative optimum self.

Exercise

Here are two ways that you can practice and incorporate meditation into your daily routine.

There are many books on meditation with many useful exercises. One of my favorites is the "Meditation and Mantras" chapter in Deepak Chopra's "Spontaneous Fulfillment of Desire: Harnessing the Infinite Power of Coincidence", published by Harmony Books. It is a wonderful read on how to meditate and incorporate mantra, a sound or vibration, into your meditation. In addition, Deepak discusses sutra which is a mantra with an ancient intention or principle that takes you deeper into your soul. Seven sutras are discussed in detail that can be combined with your daily meditation discussed above. The first sutra is listed here:

"Aham Brahmasmi"

It is followed by a more detail description,

"You are a ripple in the fabric of the cosmos. The core of my being is the ultimate reality, the root and ground of the universe, the source of all that exists"

It is followed by useful exercises on this sutra and concludes with additional information on the sutra.

Another way is to create your own meditation. Please refer to the "Recap" section above for a guideline on how and when to meditate to begin this process. Include soft music, preferably instrumental, meditative or sounds from nature – the ocean, tropical forest or rain drops are soothing to the soul – to create a peaceful ambience. Once you have completed steps 1 through 3 on page 48, write, read and imagine the following passages into your journal:

I am awake and I am alert. I have no fears, worries and anxieties. I release all negative thoughts and feelings from my body. My body is an instrument and a vessel for the universe to communicate. I need to keep my vessel clean and clear so that the universe can flow through.

I am connected with the universe. I am in harmony with life. I am guided and protected. There is a voice inside of me which has always lived. It is the voice of wisdom. This wisdom is the universal soul and I need to trust this as it guides

*me to my creative optimum self. It will lead me to the truth,
to realizing my dreams and wishes.*

*I am the creator of my life. I create the world around me
through my thoughts. My thoughts are powerful. What I see
in my mind, I see in my life. I see beauty in all things. I am
blessed with all around me. I am beauty. I am love. I am the
light of the universe. I see love everywhere. I see love in all.
We are all connected.*

Over time, this passage will evolve as you tap into your
creativity and express yourself more freely. I recommend that
you incorporate this expression into your daily meditation
and observe how it shifts your reality and connects you with
your COS.

Inspirational reading touches your soul and stirs your imagination.

STEP 3: **INSPIRATIONAL READING**

Inspirational reading is the next wonderful tool to support you on this journey. Today, there are millions of publications, books out in the market, in addition to the thousands of hours of TV that exist in our daily lives. And there are advertisements everywhere – in the subway, buses, on bill boards, everywhere you look there is information and ads of some sort. And then we have the internet and e-mail. Even with all the sophisticated pop up and e-mail filtering programs, we still receive junk mail that eats in to our available time and creates work for us. It seems everyone wants our attention. There is useful information that can be retrieved from all these vehicles of communication but our minds cannot process all this information at once and most of it is unnecessary. This creates turbulence in our thoughts rather than silence. By cluttering our minds with this kind of information, we forget who we are and we fall into the trap that we must see and process everything. If we follow this path, we disconnect from our soul.

By consciously selecting reading material that is inspirational to the mind and spirit, you can stay connected with your creative optimum self. Many wonderful poets, writers, scientists produce very inspirational publications that can help us stay connected. It does not matter the subject matter, it does matter that the reading inspires you in some way. For example, I am personally inspired by Julia Cameron, Emmet Fox and Og Mandino, to name a few. Any material that touches you deep inside, makes you feel something, stirs you inside, unleashes your imagination to pick up painting, or to call a friend, or to attend a seminar. To be inspired at this soul level is to live a complete life. Remember, we are all connected and even though on the surface we have different goals, jobs and ambitions, at the soul level, we are all the same and we want the same things. We all want to express ourselves, be appreciated and cared for and ultimately be happy. Our stories, and we all have them, are inspirational because we each have our own experiences that ultimately takes us to the same destination. We all have our unique journeys in life and it is very inspiring to learn and understand each other's journeys because we come from the same source. Here, we are one.

I remember the first time I read Kahlil Gibran's classic tale, "The Prophet", I was mesmerized by his timeless words of wisdom and knowledge. I suggest that you incorporate daily reading at a minimum once day as part of your morning ritual during journaling and meditation or when you are in the subway, after eating lunch, any time that you have a time out from the daily routine. Currently, I read a few pages from Julia Cameron's wonderful, "Heart Steps. Prayers and Declarations for a Creative Life", published by Tarcher/Putnam, as part of my morning ritual. It is a beautiful, small companion book- each page is made up inspirational words of wisdom from various writers followed by a prayer or inspiring words from Julia Cameron. The first page begins with inspirational statements from author, Sonia Choquette, followed by Julia

Cameron's own words, listed here:

> *"The universe responds to my dreams and needs. There is a unity flowing through all things. This unity is responsive to our needs. Unity responds and reacts to our positive spoken word. We are co-creative beings working with-and within-a larger whole. We embrace and contain this Source, which embraces and contains us. Drawing upon this Inner Source, we have an unlimited supply."*

As you read this, you will be inspired to write about what it means to you and explore the magic of where your writing takes you. By incorporating inspirational readings into your morning journaling and meditation, you will experience a greater connection with your creative optimum self. And as you live from this higher self, you will begin to transform your life.

Step 3 Recap: Inspirational Reading

By incorporating inspirational reading into your daily life, you still stay connected to your COS.

1. During or after meditating, select a prayer, a passage or a daily inspirational reading, about five minutes, from one of your favorite authors.
2. Be open and aware on how you feel after reading these words and write in your journal anything that comes up. You will be inspired to write about what you just read, how it relates to you and what you can learn from it. You will be amazed of new things that come up even after

reading a passage that is familiar to yo

3. Carry inspirational readings with you
   and when you feel that you are disco
   inner guide, when you mind is racing with ran.
   thoughts or if you experience anxieties or worries, take
   five minutes to read one of the passages.

Exercise

For this exercise, let's return to Julia Cameron's example I gave above. After reading the page again, take a few minutes and answer these questions into your journal. There is no correct answer here - the purpose is to see what it triggers in you to write. Write as long as you need even if the writing is not related to the question.

1. Am I aware of the power that lies underneath the word that I use in my daily life?
2. Do I consciously select the words that I use or do I say things out of habit?
3. Do I feel and believe that the universe hears my dreams and wishes? If so, when was the last time the universe fulfilled my dream?
4. What is my definition of the universe? Unity?
5. What is the Source and how do I stay connected with this Source?

Keep the answers in your journal and revisit the same questions after you have completed this book and you have incorporated the ten steps into your daily life. Note how your answers change as you continue on this journey.

Nature and solitude brings you closer to heaven on earth.

STEP 4: **NATURE AND SOLITUDE**

Nature, at its source, is innocent and wholesome with no ego. The sun just shines, the trees grow, the water flows, rain falls, birds fly – all of nature follows its own instincts and just live as they were born to be. Nature and solitude are the next steps to living The Way. These elements of nature are not worrying what others think of them. The sun does not worry if the moon will come at night. The sun and moon have trust in the universe that things will flow in the right direction so that the sun can rise and set and the moon will appear. And the same goes with the rest of the elements of nature; they have not developed the human ego and the perception of doubt. Nature is connected with the soul of the universe and it lives in peace, harmony and love. Nature lives from its creative optimum self.

As humans, we can learn from nature on how it operates and lives effortlessly. Regularly spend time with nature – it can be a walk in the park, a run along the ocean, hiking in the mountains, gazing at a beautiful landscaping or a forest, or sit by a lake and quietly observe all its elements. Observe all nature's beauty and how it allows all to live as they are born to be - there is harmony, grace and love. You see everything connected and this connection has a soul. And this is also your soul. Remember, we are all the same and when we connect to our COS we are looking at ourselves but in different forms. Because the ocean does not physically look like us, it does not mean that we are not the same. If we were not the same, we would not connect and be inspired by the ocean. Spending time with nature makes you feel safe and protected. It calms you and allows your soul to connect with the universal soul. Here, you can hear your inner voice; your guide and allows you to tap into your creativity.

The second part of this step is to regularly spend time alone. It can be for twenty minutes, a few hours, a day, a week or a month. Modern life can be overwhelming at times with work, family, friends, commitments and every day obligations that it is very easy to lose focus. When you give yourself a time out, you reconnect with your inner guide. Some people find spending time alone a big challenge. Why? They need constant stimulation from outside influences through media, people, and society in general to keep them busy and occupied and are petrified to be alone. Usually, they don't want to deal with their thoughts, feelings and worries. They think that by focusing on others, they don't need to deal with their issues. This is playing the victim and there is no room for this kind of behavior if one wishes to live their greatest life. This is also having loose ends which can be draining and blocking you from reaching your inner guide. When you choose not to deal with your issues, you are harming yourself and the world at large because you are injecting negative energy in nature. We are all connected and if we live in disorder and chaos, we create blockage to the universal flow and create delays and inefficiencies. Therefore, it is very useful to spend time alone, to recharge, regroup, re-connect with your inner guide and listen to your inner voice. This is your soul and by following it, you will have access to knowledge, wisdom and creativity.

Step 4 Recap: Nature and Solitude

By regularly spending time with nature and in solitude, you will learn more about the universe and your soul. And as you stay connected with your soul, you will gain access to infinite wisdom, intelligence and knowledge that lives in the moment.

1. Schedule time on a daily basis to spend time with nature. This can be a few minutes - walking through the park, sitting by a lake, watching birds eating, seagulls flying, waves braking on to the rocks – or more extended time as in running on the beach, hiking in the mountains or taking a bike ride through the forest.
2. As you sit with nature, live in the moment and have no other thoughts. Simply observe the elements of nature and connect with all its beauty. This will be a great time to write in your journal, meditate or read inspirational material.
3. As you connect with nature, realize that you are able to connect and enjoy what you see because you and nature are the same. You may have different forms now, but you are made up of the same energies and are exchanging them all the times. For example, oxygen in the air that we breathe.
4. Observe how this moment with nature makes you feel. You will feel peaceful. This peace that you have is available to you at all times. It lives in the moment. It is your inner

guide.

5. In addition, schedule time on a regular basis to spend time alone. This can be with nature, or just simply alone at home, write in journal, meditate, read a book, watch a movie, go sightseeing, or simply stay with your own thoughts. Do not think of anyone or anything and focus on you. You may get resistance from your ego, but in time, you will learn to appreciate your time alone. You will gain access to the silence that lives inside of you. This silence is your creative optimum self.

Exercise

Let's do a visual exercise to explore the wisdom and knowledge that is received when spending time with nature and in solitude. We can learn so much from nature and can bring that learning into our lives. Here's an example. Find a quiet, comfortable place as if you were going to meditate. Now imagine that you were in the middle of the ocean on a boat, swimming or just sitting on a barge. Visualize yourself in a safe place where you can see body of water around you and you can see the shore up ahead. Observe all the waves that surround you and notice how different each wave is – some are bigger than others, they have different shapes and wave patterns. Yet, all the waves travel together and observe how these waves move past you and head towards the shore and ultimately arrive to the shore line. All these waves are guided by the current underneath them, the invisible force that keeps all the waves together heading in one direction. Observe again how unique the waves are once they arrive to shore – some waves are bigger in size than others as they arrive to shore. Still, all the waves are fused together and all arrive together at the shore line. Now compare this observation to you and your life. Let the shore line represent your dream to be happy, to have peace, love and wisdom in your life, and to have all your dreams realized. And let you be one of these waves traveling together, in harmony, with billions of other waves, or people. We are all aiming for the same goal, the shore line, but we choose different paths to get there. Still, there is an invisible force, the soul, that keeps us all together to realize all our dreams. It is your choice to stay connected to your COS, navigate harmoniously through life and arrive at the same destination which is living your greatest life.

Well being makes you a shining star.

STEP 5: **WELL BEING**

Now that you are practicing journaling, meditation, inspirational reading and spending time with nature and alone on a regular basis, you will become more aware of how you feel about yourself and the world around you. Your senses are heightened as you become an observer of your thoughts and peel away all the layers that have accumulated over time due to social conditioning. As you peel away these layers, it is important to be kind to yourself and to forgive the things that have upset you in the past. The past no longer exists and the present is always available to have a new start, and this new start begins by taking care of yourself and your overall well being. Taking better care of your body with the kind of food and drinks that you partake, in forms of exercise you choose, rest and handling every day stress will bring you closer to living from your COS.

Optimal well being needs to be part of your daily life and it begins with realizing that your body is precious to you and need to take responsibility to treat it kindly. As you know, the body is a very complex, intricate and beautiful temple that works mostly on its own. It does not require your assistance in the millions of scientific tasks that the cells in your body perform on a daily basis. Anyone who has taken a biology class knows that the body is simply magical in its abilities, intelligence and wisdom. You don't need to tell the cells how to process food, protect you from disease, heal your wounds, breathe air and a million of other things – it automatically does them. The only responsibility that we have is to treat it kindly and this is where sometimes problems arise.

Because we have a choice on what to eat, drink, and how we live our lives, the choices we make impact how the body performs. If we don't treat it kindly and choose not to take responsibility for these actions to correct them, issues come up with our bodies. For the most part, this is how addictions to food, alcohol, drugs and many others begin. People can give many reasons why they choose to get drunk, become obese or rely on stimulants, and in their mind, these reasons can be justified. Ultimately, if you go deep with the person and go to the source to why they choose to have this kind of addiction, you will find that the person has chosen, at least for the time being, to abuse their body. They have lost respect for themselves - it is a choice they are making and at any time they can make a new choice and change things around. That is the magic of our bodies, if bad choices are replaced with more conscious, well being choices, the body will heal itself. It is very important to be aware and realize that we have a responsibility to treat our body kindly so that it can functional at its optimal level.

Sometimes, we can easily be influenced by society, parents, cultures, and media on what they think we should be eating. I was born and grew up in an Italian family, and eating is a big part of our culture. I appreciate how Italians, and many other cultures share the same tradition in dedicating a whole day on creating the perfect meal. Growing up there were so many delicious meals that one day a friend made me realize that all we did is think about food and "we live to eat". The whole day was spent on what to eat, how to prepare it and who to invite. While sharing delicious meals was and still is beautiful today, I realized that my family was focusing too much on eating. And as a result, I ate larger portions that I needed it to. Today, I "eat to live optimally" – a different approach that focuses on what the body needs rather than what families, culture, traditions and society say we should eat. And the body does give clues on what it needs to be optimal. We just need to listen.

The body tells us what it needs to function at its best. Scientists tell us that the body is made up of about 60% of water, so it comes to no surprise that the body loves fresh water. The body is also made up of cells that needs nutrients to function properly and these same natural nutrients are found in plants and fruits. It comes to no surprise that the body loves fresh fruits, vegetables and legumes. Cells also need other nutrients, as in protein and fat, and this can be found in plants and animals. The body needs these nutrients to operate at its best as the body works continuously 24 hours a day - but it requires more nutrients when we are awake then when we are sleeping because we expend more energy when we are awake. It makes sense to spread out what we eat during our waking hours and not eat right before sleeping because the body needs to work to digest the food and it may keep us awake.

Depending on our genes and how we were raised, bodies vary on specific foods that it needs to perform at its best. It is important for each of us to understand what specific foods we can intake to make us feel good. There are many diet books and experts that advise us what we should eat to stay healthy and to lose weight. There is agreement among experts that food and drink that are either not fresh and natural, processed based are not healthy. And your body, the ultimate expert, will tell you that this is not healthy by making you feel lethargic, heavy and giving you discomfort. If we know this, and we do because most of all our foods and drinks today have labels, we can choose not to eat or drink them. What then should we eat and drink? You can receive good guidance from many diet plans, nutritional experts and doctors. Still, the best expert is your body. A great way to better understand this is to keep a food journal where you record what you eat, the amounts and very importantly, how you feel afterwards.

The body will "speak" after eating in terms of how you feel in your stomach, you mind and your overall energy. You can learn if you are allergic to some foods or if some foods make you tired. For example, if I eat pasta during lunch, it makes me sleepy and makes it harder for me to continue with my work for the rest of the day. My breakfast is made up fresh berries, grapefruit, banana, yogurt and whole grains. If I eat pancakes, eggs, or any other breakfast items, my mind does not feel right. It feels lethargic and "cloudy". Now that I am aware of how these foods make me feel I can choose foods that keep me awake and energetic. You can do the same by keeping a food journal for a month or two to learn which foods will keep your body at its optimal state. You will learn what to eat and how much so that your body can function at its best.

Eating the right foods will help you maintain the ideal body weight. There are useful charts that indicate how much one should weight based on the sex, age and height. If you monitor your weight on a regular basis, your body will guide you to find the optimal level. Naturally, how you enjoy your food is also a key component in optimal well being. Sharing meals with friends and loved ones should be a joyous, harmonious and peaceful experience. As you prepare to eat your food, it is important to remember and to be consciously aware that you are not only nourishing your body with energy from food but also with energy from your environment. It is important that your environment maintains a positive energy so that this same wonderful energy enters the body. For example, everyone can feel the difference between sharing a peaceful and happy meal, compared to a meal when there are arguments among the guests. Arguments generate resentments, anxieties and frustrations and these emotions carry hostile energies. If you allow these bad energies to enter your body, it creates discomfort. This has a greater impact when you are eating because the body not only needs to work on digesting your food but it needs to work more in dealing with stress that has enter the body.

For example, growing up my father, at times, had a bad temper and during dinner, there were arguments with my mother and sometimes it unfortunately got physical. Luckily, I was there at times to intervene and stop the situation from worsening but I remember that I always felt drained and had stomachaches afterwards. The body was complaining. We can change this. Just like we consciously choose the kind of foods we eat, we can choose a warm and gracious location, and the right people we share it with. Watching TV should be limited because it takes the attention away from the food you are enjoying and the people you are sharing it with. If you are eating alone, still take pleasure in creating a warm environment for yourself whether you listen to music or sit by the lake while eating your lunch. If you create a warm and gracious environment while eating, you will nurture the body with wonderful energy for it to perform at its best.

Another way to keep the body at its optimal state is through a regular exercise program. Everyone needs to consult with their doctor before performing any exercise or engaging in any type of exercise program to discuss any limitations the body may have to certain type of exercises. In general, everyone agrees that exercise helps the body to stay in shape, and when the body is in good shape, it can perform well and makes you feel good. We have a choice and a responsibility to keep the body at an optimal level. Similar to foods, there are a variety of exercises that one can choose from. The best way to understand what works best for you is to journal how you feel afterwards.

If you observe closely, you will notice a difference in how you feel after performing different types of exercises. For example, if you play a team sport like soccer, you will experience a connection with everyone because the game is based on synchronicities, strategy and execution with the team. If you bike outdoors for a long ride, you will experience that all is possible and within your reach because of the expansive scenery and views you experience while traveling at a faster speed. If you use an indoor elliptical machine, it will give you an overall workout because you are using many parts of the body and it will make you feel complete. If you swim in a lap pool or ocean, you will grace the water with precision as the water soothes your body and soul. Regardless of the exercise you choose, the overall body and mind will feel better. You will receive more creative ideas and solutions to problems while exercising and you will have more energy, clarity and feel lighter. Record your observations in your journal and learn which exercises work best for you and your body.

Listening to your body when it needs rest and sleep are important to keep the body at its optimal state of being. We don't need to be scientists to know all the details why sleep and rest is important, but we know that if we do not give our bodies enough rest, it will not function at its best. You feel sluggish, confused, and have greater anxieties and worry about things more easily when you don't get enough rest. And how much rest do you need? Studies show that it varies with people, but the general consensus is between 7-8 hours a day. Some people feel at their best when they go to sleep by 10pm and are up before 6am. Sometimes this is not possible due to life situations and the body can adapt. You need to observe and try it for yourself what works best.

For years now, I no longer use an alarm clock to wake up when I go to sleep at a regular time. The body knows when it has received enough sleep and wakes up. And there are times that for different reasons, the body needs less sleep. For example, as I wrote the first draft of this book on a daily basis, I slept no more than four hours. I would wake up in the middle of the night, thinking about what to write, and decided to get up and write. I knew that I would be awake all night and would not be able to sleep. Why would I choose not to get up, if the body is telling me to get up? The body speaks to us, we just need to listen. And if the body has aches and pains, a body massage will do wonders. Experiment with a wide range of body and holistic services that exist today and see what works best for you. If you learn to listen to your body and give it your attention, the body will be able to work for you at its optimal level.

When you are connected and listen to your body, you form a bond, an intimate special relationship. The body speaks to you, through signs of comfort and discomfort, what to eat and drink, what exercise to perform and how much you should do and how much rest you need on a particular day.

The body is an intricate, complex and intelligent being with full of wisdom and ready to teach us. It is our responsibility to follow the body's guidance and make choices that will keep it performing at its best. By performing at its optimal, it will allow you to stay connected with your soul and it will guide you to transform yourself and the world by living from your creative optimum self.

Step 5 Recap: Well Being

Taking great care of your body is an important step to achieve a better life.

1. Realize that you have been blessed with a body that is complex, intelligent and full of wisdom. The body performs millions of activities without requiring, for the most part, your input. When the body needs your participation, as in what to eat, it is your responsibility to consciously make choices that will provide comfort to your body.
2. Keep a food journal and record what and how much you eat and drink and how you feel afterwards. Eat foods that are fresh, natural and earthy and make you feel strong, energetic and give you clarity. Refrain from foods that are processed, artificial and chemical based and make you feel lethargic, heavy and foggy.
3. Use the weight chart as a guideline to what your ideal body weight should be. As you learn more about the food you eat and how it impacts your body, you will find the ideal weight and body fat measurement that is optimal for you.
4. Create a warm and gracious environment when you eat

and keep your attention on the food that you are enjoying.

5. Maintaining an active life through regular exercise is essential in keeping your body at its optimal state. You need to consult with your doctor first, but choose exercises that makes you feel lighter and energetic, releases stress and gives you a connection to the universe. Vary your exercises so that you look forward to performing them and become an exciting, integral part of your day.

6. Giving your body proper rest is an essential part in overall well being. For most people, about 8 hours work best for most of the time, but you should experiment yourself what works best for you. If you listen to your body, it will guide you when to wake up and how much rest it needs on a particular day. Treat your body to a massage when you are having aches and pains. It will do wonders for you.

Exercise

Food journaling is a useful exercise to understand the foods to eat, what kind of exercise to perform and how much rest the body needs. For a month, record in a journal on each day the following information:

- Type of food and drink and the respective amount and the time of day
- How did you feel afterwards? Did you feel heavy, bloated, foggy, lethargic, energetic, happy, sad, worry? Be very specific
- Type of exercise you performed on that day, the length of

time and the time you performed it.

- How did you feel during the exercise? What were you thinking of? Did you come up with a solution to a problem you had? Did you get creative ideas on wanting to do something? Were you visualizing your dreams? Be very specific
- Record what time you woke up, and how did you feel? Were you foggy, tired, energetic, awake? Do you remember any dreams and if so what were they?
- Record what time you went to bed at night and did you fall asleep right away or did you have any thoughts?

As you now know, journaling is a useful tool to understand and learn about yourself. Try this for a month and you will learn more about your body on the type of foods, the kind of exercise and the amount of rest it needs to live at its optimal state. When you body functions at its best, you will be connected with your COS.

Transforming your world is within your reach.

PART III

TRANSFORM YOUR WORLD

The five *inner* steps that you just completed will guide you to be more open and aware of everything around you. As you execute these steps on a regular basis and over time, you will see a transformation in your life as you live from your COS. You will have more positive energy, feel and look younger and be more in-tune with your body and life around you. As you interact with the rest of the world, people will begin to notice a change in you. This brings us to the five *outer* steps that you need to ensure that your transformation continues on this journey.

The *outer* steps are living with no loose ends, nurture all relationships, be warm and gracious, be passionate and grateful and live from your COS with eyes and ears of the universe.

Outer steps are grounded in truth, honor and order.

CHAPTER SIX

INSPIRATION FOR *OUTER* STEPS

The *outer* steps are inspired by the years of success I experienced in the business world. Business or any type of work is part of life. If we can succeed in one part of life, business in this case, we can leverage what we have learned that works and incorporate it into other parts of our lives. The five *outer* steps are based on the five principles that I have used successfully in all my work with companies, clients and family business.

From delivering espresso at five years old to delivering Creative Optimum Solutions to Wall Street firms, the project and the people may change but the principles to succeed remain the same. I have worked with people from all professions, walks of life, across many industries and all level of management. During my career, I have worked on wide range of projects – from complex, high profile, multi billion dollar initiatives to smaller, one month projects. I have mastered the five principles or keys to succeed in any type of work.

The five principles are efficiency, proactive communication, flexible process, leadership & execution and creativity. With these principles, I have successfully executed a wide range of projects and initiatives and as a result, clients have reaped the benefits from the work in terms of reduced costs, increase in productivity, sales and profits. When I expanded my consulting practice and included personal transformation workshops, I turned to these same principles for guidance in developing five *outer* steps for personal and social transformation. I leveraged what works in one part of life to assist in transforming another part of life.

Each of the five *outer* steps are derived and related to the five business principles. When you live with no loose ends, you have order in your life, less clutter in your mind and in your environment. There is efficiency. The next *outer* step is to nurture all relationships which is the same as developing and maintaining solid business relationships. Thirdly, be warm and gracious implies that you are respectful and flexible with all your worldly interactions. The next *outer* step is to be passionate and grateful which are also two key qualities of a successful business leader. And the final *outer* step is to live from your COS which implies unlimited creativity in all that you do.

There you have it – the relationship and the connections between the *outer* steps and the business principles. Let's get started and execute the *outer* steps.

Executing the outer steps will make the universal dreams come true.

CHAPTER 7

EXECUTE THE *OUTER* STEPS

Now that you have the source of inspiration for the *outer* steps, let me show you how you can incorporate these steps into your daily life and transform your world. Each step concludes with a written or visual exercise. I recommend that you complete each exercise the first time through and revisit them at a later time to observe and compare changes with the results.

Live with no loose ends and you flow everywhere.

STEP 6: **LIVE WITH NO LOOSE ENDS**

As you incorporate the *inner* steps into your daily life you are more connected with your inner guide and more comfortable "in your own skin". You are more aware and ready to learn from your experiences, have more knowledge, wisdom and curiosity about the world around you. This curiosity pushes you to interact more with the world leading to the first *outer* step – living with no loose ends. This is a powerful way to gain more access to the inner wisdom inside of you because there will be less clutter in the way. I define a loose end this way: when you intentionally say or write that you will do or say something that is "positive" in nature and then you don't follow through. There are many people who choose to live this way and over time, this kind of living creates stress, anxiety and toxic relationships. It creates clutter, extra baggage and inefficiencies everywhere. If you have a loose end in your mind - you said you were going to make a phone call last week, pay your bills, schedule an appointment, write a poem or begin writing a book but you did not follow through, your mind is occupied in worrying about these things and prevents you from living in the moment. When you are not living in the moment, you miss out on life because you are not truly connected with your creative optimum self. And when you are not connected, your life is not as joyous, not as peaceful and not as blissful as it can be. As a result, when you interact with people, you will express the same anxiety, confusion and stress, and the world suffers.

But the world can be transformed when we live with no loose ends. Similar to the first *inner* step and journaling, this first *outer* step is difficult for most people because they are not aware how this kind of living creates extra work for everyone. A simple example is the following – you are able to make a "hard to get" reservation at a fancy restaurant on Valentine's day. The host asks you to please call if you need to cancel as there is a long waiting list. Your plans change and you decide to go somewhere else or more likely stay home and celebrate. Like most people, you do not call and cancel the reservation. As a result, the restaurant is probably left with an empty table at that time, even though there is a waiting list. Now, on this list, there was a couple who would pay any price to eat at this restaurant because it is their favorite and they are celebrating their anniversary. Your choice of not calling to cancel the reservation had a domino effect – the restaurant possibly lost revenue, the service staff earned less that night, and the anniversary couple was probably disappointed. If you kept your word and called, others would have benefited. Usually the universe, with its eternal power, has a way of working things out for the better when we are faced with inconveniences. Still, we can do our part to create harmony in these situations. There is a universal order in life and if you intend to do something positive and do not follow through, you create disorder. And the universe needs to work on your behalf to correct the situation.

Here's another example of how coincidences and living with no loose ends can lead to new opportunities. One time, I met a guy at the health club and we connected on the spot. We discussed about going biking together and I told him that I will e-mail him with a time that we can go together. Days go by and I did not follow through. Each time I revisit the club and other places in the city, I would run into him and each time I am reminded that I have not followed through. It's as if the universe is reminding me of my loose end and it is giving me a clue that it is important that I connect with him - I will learn something new or it is an invitation to a new experience. The universe has ears and eyes and when I make an intention and do not follow through, I get reminders, like you get from online calendar reminders. I finally followed through and we went on our bike ride and learned that he was a major player at a top financial company that I wanted to do business with. We became good friends which led to a long term engagement with his company.

And writing this book became a very big loose end in my life. One day, I was discussing with Tanya the benefits of living with no loose ends and she turns to me and says that I am living with the "biggest loose end - write your book." I would talk about writing my book for almost two years, we brainstormed but never sat down to write it. I always put other priorities first, my clients or family. Every day I was reminded of my loose end from the same people who encouraged me to write the book as they thought it is an inspiring message that needs to be delivered. Still, I hesitated, until the universe had to intervene on a grander scale. Over two months, three large business deals in a row fell through at the last moment due to unforeseen circumstances. Now, I no longer had excuses, the business work went away which allowed me to sit down and write this book. Once I began writing, I could not stop until

I was finished. The universe receives the credit for intervening and orchestrating the events that allowed me to follow through on my intention.

The internet and all of the advanced technology makes living in the moment with no loose ends much easier. We can stay connected via e-mail, messaging and the internet on our phones and portable devices. Everything is at our fingertips. As a result, we can be more efficient and accomplish more by "tying up" all loose ends during the day. As a result, we are left with an empty mind or vessel, as they say in the arts, ready to be inspired by all of life. This source of inspiration is all around us when we live in the moment and with no loose ends.

Step 6 Recap: Live with No Loose Ends

Live your life with no loose ends and you will gain access to the inner wisdom that lives all around you. Here's how you can make sure that you are living with no loose ends.

1. Make a daily list of things you need to do that day. Prioritize everything and cross it off when you complete the items.
2. Review the list on a daily basis to ensure that the items truly belong on this list, or they are more long term goals and should be kept on a long term project list. For example, buying a home can take months, so it should not be on the daily list. However, contacting several realtors to begin the process of buying a home should be on the daily list.

3. Record in your journal how you feel when you complete an item or when you still have items on the list that you have not completed. This observation will make you more aware of things and will give you greater access to the inner wisdom that lives inside of you.

Exercise

Try this simple exercise. Make a complete list of all the things you said you were going to do. Include everything – bills you said you need to pay, calls you need to make, classes you want to take, a home you wish to buy one day. For each item on the list, give it a date that you will complete this item and place this list somewhere in your home or with you so you are visually reminded each day. Update the list by crossing off items completed and each time you have a new "to do", add it to this list. I keep my list on my blackberry and I update it during the day. As you practice with this over time, you will experience more clarity in your mind, you will be more open to creativity and source of inspiration and you will have more energy. Now, you can use this extra energy to nurture all of your relationships, which is the next *outer* step.

Nurturing all relationships will cleanse and rejuvenate your soul.

STEP 7: **NURTURE ALL RELATIONSHIPS**

As you begin to incorporate living with no loose ends into your daily life, you will be more connected with your inner guide. You will be more aware of who you truly are, curious of the world around and connected to the universe. You will begin to realize that your thoughts, words and actions impact your life, those around you and the rest of the world. You will have more clarity in your life, order in your mind and home and energy to share. You are transforming yourself. This transformation continues by realizing the value of all of your relationships, which bring us to the next *outer* step and nurturing all of your relationships. As you respect, love and are honest with all of your relationships, you will learn more about yourself and people around and you will guide others to find their COS.

By living this way, you will have a better understanding that you are truly connected with the rest of the world. Remember that the earth is spinning so fast in space that our eyes can not see our connection, but we truly are one with one another and the universe - your thoughts and actions have an impact. If you choose to be open and nurture your relationships, the rest of the world will be inspired to give the same respect, love and honesty and together we can have a better world. It does not cost anything to live this way and the payoff is priceless because you will feel elated as you express kindness or compassion. It is your natural state. You feel lighter and warm inside, like the sun – it just feels right.

Nurture all your relationships - relationship you have with your self, your family, friends and adversaries, community, government, foreigners, business colleagues, the environment, nature and even the so-called "evil" people in this world. Most people may have a difficult time understanding the idea of respecting an "evil" person, but remember that even though we appear or behave differently, at the soul level, we are all the same. If you live from this place and your actions are fueled by this knowledge, then you can even show some compassion or understanding to someone who has temporarily lost the connection to universal goodness.

We already discussed nurturing your self or well being – eating the right foods, exercising regularly, getting plenty of rest. This is not a selfish act as some people may think, but rather the right thing to do if you want to be a guiding light and inspiration for others. If you nurture your body and mind first and make it optimal, you will then be able to provide that goodness, love and harmony to others and the world. It is all about having great, harmonious energy and if you have that first in yourself, you will then be able to provide this to others.

It has taken me a long time to understand this. Growing up, I assumed the role of a caretaker. My primary focus was to take care of others and bring harmony into their lives. I would break up arguments in my home between my parents and bring more peace and harmony to the situation; I would solve other people's problems, or just fix what was broken. And even though I felt better that I was helping others, there was little energy available to take care of my needs. Today, I continue to assist others but I do it from a stronger part of myself. I know who I am first and I take care of my needs and as a result, my actions and intentions come from a stronger self and universal truth. My energy is stronger, more healing and transforming.

Nurturing your family is an important relationship that will guide you to learn more about your self and the world around you. If you stay connected with your family over the years, you will realize that your parents are more than just parents, they are human beings just like you are. They have dreams, goals, experience fears and anxieties, and they also have a soul. This soul comes from the same place as yours. If you can look at your family at this level, you will have more understanding and compassion for who they are. This compassion will help you to understand when you have different opinions about things or when you see things within your family that are just not right.

Growing up, I was very close with both of my parents, but I had a different relationship with each one. I looked up to my father and learned great deal of business and life wisdom, but I also observed that he had a temper and a short fuse. Although I was never physically abused from my father, the same can not be said of my mother and brother. When I witnessed these events, I always intervened, stopped the ugly occurrences, and worked to bring a level of peace to the situation. I could see that my father loved my mom and his elder son very much but at times he was not able to control his anger. He was not able to handle the stress of his life and he knew no other way of dealing with it then to get physical. When I was young I was not strong enough to speak to my father about this, but as I got older in my teens I stood up to him more. I would tell him that it was wrong how he handled things, I was truthful with him, and over time, the arguments were less frequent. Eventually, my father did find peace with himself and was able to control and stop the abuse. Before he died at the young age of 57, he reconciled his differences with my mom and brother. But, this was costly. If I or the rest of my family had addressed this issue early on, we would have shared more peaceful and loving experiences without carrying the "expensive" baggage.

The relationship with my mother was more whole-some and it still is today. Growing up, I learned a great deal of wisdom that I still use today in my life. She is the most amazing and courageous person that I have ever met, a great inspiration. After I graduated high school, I realized that our relationship was changing. I was becoming more independent and relied less on her guidance and wisdom. As a mother, she did not like this idea as she always wanted to take care of things. But after my father died she became depressed and very ill and now the tables were reversed. I became the care taker. Over time, she lost all her independence, she relied on a walker for mobility and a home support worker to bathe and dress her. She complained of having constant pain in her body even though the doctors were not able to diagnose the source of her pain. Still, I continued to give her love and respect while I shared my concerns that this was not healthy for both of us. I spoke the truth. Today, my mom is 73 years "young" and continues to transform. She has regained most of her in-dependence and is healthy – she runs on the beach and swims in the pool. It is joy to watch her live again and she credits my support and the same ten steps described here for guiding her to reconnect with her inner guide.

Sometimes, you may need to go separate ways but true love will always return. My brother and I were very close growing up, he was my best friend. And it wasn't until we got older and in my 20's did I pick up friction in our relationship. The friction was based on the fact that I was not his little brother anymore and did not rely on him as much. I was growing up but my brother still wanted to take care of things for me. And then once he married, we grew apart. Still, at the soul level we still loved each other very much. When my brother was not experiencing a healthy marriage, I was there to support him and told him the truth about his toxic relationship. But he didn't want to accept it; as a result we didn't have a relationship for a long time. Today, my brother is on a way to regain his true identity. He is going through a divorce after a long and difficult marriage and is evolving every day reconnecting with his creative optimum self.

An intimate relationship will evolve over time as you both grow and transform your individual needs while supporting each other with unconditional love. Tanya and I have gone through many changes in our lives - we have grown so much together and we both credit the fact that above all we respect each other as human beings first and we are honest with our feelings. It does not take much to be kind to your loved ones. You will not agree with everything but if you understand why they feel the way they do, give them the respect they deserve as a human being and be truthful with how you feel, you will have a healthy relationship. It may take some time, and it is possible that you will realize that you are not capable of sharing time or living together anymore and need to go your separate ways. You are each making choices that do not provide the harmony that you need in a healthy relationship. If you are not able to work out a compromise why stay together and be miserable. Be respectful, show compassion and truth and you will arrive at the right solution because you will be connected with your inner guide. You will have the wisdom and knowledge to take the next appropriate steps.

As you extend this unconditional love with all the children in your life, whether or not they are part of your family, you will appreciate their innate wisdom and learn a few things from them as well. Children, by nature, are born innocent and pure - "clean" of any judgments, labels or preconceived notions about people or things. They need guidance and support to "learn" how to operate in this life and a loving and harmonious environment to grow into mature human and spiritual beings. Some people forget this and choose to treat children with little respect as if they are not "old enough" to know about life, not smart enough to learn a new skill or wise enough to make the right decision. Unfortunately, some situations turn for the worse as some resort to violence to defend their opinion, discipline or demonstrate their authoritative power over the children. As children experience these sufferings, they accumulate layers of fears, anger and low self worth around their beautiful souls as they grow. They are not happy with their lives - don't like their job, have no passion for simple things in life, and attract people who have the same toxic energy as their parents. Some are lucky enough to realize this and dedicate most of their adult life to transform by peeling and removing away all these layers and reconnect with their soul. Others are not so lucky – they treat their own children with the same unhealthy ways and contribute to the sufferings experienced today by some children. This needs to stop once and for all! We can all do this by nurturing all children with the love and respect that they deserve and provide a harmonious environment for them to mature beautifully.

As you extend this respect, compassion and honesty to your friends, you will gain more wisdom and knowledge about life as you become a source of inspiration. There are various types of friendships – those that you share a very special bond and you are intimate, those that you only share some time together because you are physically apart, friends that you have known your entire life but have grown apart and rarely have time for each other. Regardless of the length of time that you share together and the level of intimacy, you can still be soulful. You may have different professional titles, amount of money, or interests, but you understand and appreciate who they are. This is real love and nothing can separate this. As you open yourself up and show this kind of love and respect they will do the same because you are connecting at a deeper level, where all is understood. Celebrate all your friends, their various interests and backgrounds, and when you share time together, either in person, phone or e-mail, be honorable, be respectful and you will connect with your own soul that lives in them. You will experience a warm feeling inside and you will create magical moments together.

Even your so-called adversaries deserve the same kind of respect. Why? Because an adversary is a label created by society and the ego to differentiate ourselves from someone who has a different political, religious, business or any other type of belief from us. We consider adversaries our enemies because their thoughts differ and we think they do not deserve the same kind of attention that we give our true friends. But your friends may change and adopt new beliefs so they may become your adversaries one day and vice versa. Your current adversaries can grow and become your friends one day as they share more of your vision. And you may learn a great deal from these adversaries as well, but if you don't share and give the respect that they deserve, as a human being, you will never know this. I have seen this so many times in life that as I open up with all people, I learn a great deal more about myself, the other person and life in general. And it does not cost us anything.

Even the so-called "evil" people in the world can benefit from our understanding and compassion and in turn they will transform and improve their lives. You may ask yourself how can you respect someone who has taken another life or has committed a brutal crime? There is no tolerance for this type of crime and an appropriate action is necessary to ensure that these crimes are not committed. However, the current punishment system is not working, because if it did there will be no more crimes in the world. And there would be no more "evil" people today but they still exist. Maybe the problem is that we need to understand why these people are doing what they are doing. In their mind, they are doing the right thing. Naturally something has gone wrong with their thinking, the way they were raised, and how they live their lives. They are not happy and do not know how to express themselves and resort to violence. In a way, society supports violence as in a war; there is a winner and a loser. No one wishes to lose so they fight hard and kill more people to achieve victory. But how does this solve the bigger problem of finding a permanent solution? It doesn't and there will never be one unless we understand why people do what they did in the first place so that it can be rectified in the long run.

We need to have a more soulful approach to deal with hostile situations. We need to remember that they were not born "evil" but something has gone wrong in their lives and they are choosing to act this way. We all have done wrongful things in our lives, maybe not so extreme to have someone label us as "evil", but we all have done things that have caused emotional or physical pain to someone. But as we learn more about ourselves, grow in wisdom and knowledge and stay connected with our creative optimum self, we transform into beings that have respect for life, love for all and are truthful in all ways. If we can transform, then it is possible that everyone else can. This possibility is real and it takes each of us to do our part and live a life of respect and kindness.

As you go beyond the wrongdoing of what an "evil" person has done, you will see that they have a soul that needs to live. They may have temporarily lost the connection with their soul, as we have in the past, but the soul is still there. They need to reconnect with their soul, and go on a journey similar to everyone. If we can truly understand this and allow it to govern our actions when designing real and practical solutions to this problem, we can assist these people to find their lost soul and reconnect with their inner guide. One solution is to transform the "fabric" of society by incorporating steps discussed in this book or similar steps that inspire and empower people to live their full potential. As this becomes part of every day living, including in schools and businesses, we will see a shift from evil to more harmony in the world. It may take some time, but it is worth the journey for a more peaceful future.

As you live in your community, be conscious of the needs of the community, volunteer your time to a worthy cause, open the door for someone, assist the elderly with the groceries, smile at everyone's eyes, be thankful of all that you have, greet everyone by their names, say thank you and please. Good karma feeds on itself; you create your community by the energy that you give. Be courteous, kind, and show your soul to the community and in turn you will get the same soul back. Some people think that just because you are paying for a service it is OK to be disrespectful. They think that money buys the right to be unkind. If they live this kind of life, they are ultimately poor. Bad karma will catch up with this kind of living. There is a universal, orderly flow of energy – good and bad - and one receives what one gives. Therefore, why would anyone want to give bad energy? Be wise. Live from the same soul when you interact with all people. Be kind to your waitress, bus driver, banker, if someone says thank you instead of responding "no problem", consider, "you are welcome" or "my pleasure to assist". Saying "no problem" indicates that there was a problem from the beginning. If you think about it, "no problem" is improperly used at times. It separates us. Express the same love to a stranger as you show your loved ones and you will learn new things about life and new opportunities will flow your way.

When you travel to foreign places, be curious of the culture and appreciate the way they live. Don't assume that they will speak your spoken language and remember that the power of the unspoken word. Be aware and learn about new places, new foods, different parts of the world. Show your respect and kindness and the world will open the door to new experiences. You will be embraced by foreign lands, feel safe and protected and make new friends. You will feel like you were home because at the moment you will be living from your soul and when you live from that place you are authentic. As you work and conduct business affairs, live from the same place. It does not matter what your profession is, be respectful, kind and truthful and you will reap the benefits of good karma. Some people think that they need to act different when at work - they can not be the same, they need to hide their feelings or can not be truthful. This causes inefficiencies in the work place. Bring your soul to work and not only will you be much happier but you will help create harmony, inspire others to do the same and, as a result, your company will be more efficient. You will be more productive and an inspiration to others to follow in your footsteps. Great ideas often emerge from an environment where people are able to express themselves, share their vision and are truthful.

Nurture your relationship with your government by showing respect; be truthful with your needs and work together to create policies that are most beneficial to everyone. In the United States, there is a low, voter turn-out during presidential, senatorial and other elections because people think that there is a lack of good candidates to choose from. As a result, many people do not exercise the right to vote and a candidate is elected president who does not represent the majority of the citizens. We are blessed to live in a democratic country that gives its people the right to vote and select leaders most qualified to create effective programs for everyone. We need to exercise this right by voting and making a statement on what is important in our country and who we think is the right candidate. There are talented people that will serve the country well, but because of the lack of media, the "old school" way of thinking, or the "politics" of government they are not elected. If we develop honest relationships with our government officials, we will guide government to work for our best interest. We need to speak up when programs and policies designed to promote peace and fairness in our society are not working. Over time, as more people are involved and participate in these relationships, the government agencies will transform, they have no choice. And as our government transforms, our actions will inspire and assist governments in other countries to do the same.

Nurture your environment and you will create a harmonious and efficient world around you. Clean up after yourself when using a public table, a park or beach area, after using the treadmill or bike at the health club, and don't litter because when you do, you are creating additional work for someone else. How would you feel if someone created more work for you? Be conscious of how you live your life inside and outside of your home and make choices that bring harmony and efficiency to nature and all its environment. If we are open, we can learn a great deal from nature and we may be surprised by the many teachers we may find along the way.

A beautiful, Pekingese dog named Bianco taught me the meaning of "living in the moment". Bianco was an old soul and I would watch him every morning at about the same time, go outside to our beautiful, large garden. He would go out a few times during the day, even during a snow storm, and each time he went out he would go around and smell every flower, branch or leaf. It was as if he was looking at it for the first time. I sat there watching him and I realized how beautiful his world was. He was excited to be out there and always experienced it as the first time. That is living in the moment, with no labels, judgments or preconceived notions. By living in the moment, you can learn, become inspired and experience new joys.

Step 7 Recap: Nurture All Relationships

Here's a recap on how nurturing all of your relationships will bring wisdom into your life.

1. Nurture all relationships begins by showing respect, love and honesty with yourself. Realize that by nurturing your

self first, you will gain more knowledge to who you are and what you need to be happy. By having a healthy relationship with your self, you will then be able to develop and maintain other relationships based on the same trust.

2. Extend your love and understanding to your family and you will be a source of inspiration for your family to transform their lives. It may take some time for some people to take the first step to make a change in their lives but with your honesty and guidance, they will connect with their soul.

3. Express unconditional love to your loved ones and all the children in the world and you will be rewarded with deep relationships that go beyond this life time.

4. Nurture the relationships with your friends and adversaries and you will mature and gain great wisdom. Realize that you will not connect with all of your friends the same way, but seek out opportunities to learn something new from all of your friends. As you show respect and understanding with your adversaries, you may realize that your ideas may not be so distant and your adversary may become your friend one day.

5. It takes wisdom and maturity to realize that even the "evil" people in the world need our understanding and support to inspire them into a better life. Understand that these people have disconnected temporarily from their soul but the possibility exists that they will be able to reconnect with their higher self. By implementing programs based on practical solutions, including the *inner* and *outer* steps discussed here, we can create a better world for everyone.

6. Nurture your community, government, be kind to people you meet on the streets, daily interactions you have with neighbors, service professionals and all the people you interact on the phone and internet, and the people you

meet in your travels. Show respect and kindness and you will have an opportunity to learn more about yourself through these relationships. When you connect with people at the soul level, you move the world into a higher state of living. You align yourself with the flow of life and all of the goodness of the universe.

7. Nurture your environment and nature and you will create harmony in the world. Be responsible and make daily conscious choices that assist in keeping the environment clean, safe and orderly and you will inspire others to do the same. Show gratitude and appreciate the relationship you have with nature and all its creatures and you will gain more knowledge and wisdom. Always be aware and have a thirst for curiosity and learning and nature will reward you by teaching you how to live in the moment. When you learn to live in the moment, you will be connected with your creative optimum self and as you continue to live from the source, you will be transforming your self and the world at the same time.

Exercise

This exercise may take a few days to complete and it may last over a period of time but it is very powerful with the results you will observe. Follow these steps and watch transformation in action.

1. In a journal make a list of all your groups of relationships. The groups are: your self, your family, friends, adversaries, business colleagues, "evil" people, community, service professionals, foreigners, environment, nature.

2. For each group, make a list of names of all the people in that group. For example, for the community, make a list of all your neighbors, doorman, taxi driver and the rest of the people that live and work in your community, including a sub group called strangers. Under environment, include streets, stores, and other public spaces.

3. For each of the names in the group, write down what you can do to show respect, understanding, kindness or honesty to each. Keep the action item simple and practical. For example, for an adversary, an act of kindness can be to simply ask questions and try to understand their point of view. Or for your lover, you can write a poem. For your business colleague, you can assist with their project. For a stranger, you can assist with driving directions.

4. Now that you have a list of action items, put it to practice. Next time you interact with your relationships, follow through with an action item. For those people that you will probably not interact with, visualize following through with an action item next time you meditate.

5. As you follow through with your actions, be aware of the experience that it generates. You will understand that everyone wants to be understood, wants compassion, love, truth and honesty. We all want and need the same things and it does take much effort or cost anything to give this. All we need is the commitment from everyone to do their part. In this way, we can graciously transform the world.

Be warm and gracious and your glow will warm the earth.

STEP 8: **BE WARM AND GRACIOUS**

As you appreciate and nurture all your relationships, you understand that your existence is valuable to the world and your thoughts and actions have an impact on your life. You know that living from your creative optimum self is the only way to live because at this level all worries and anxieties will diminish. You may still experience moments of weakness, but you will be able to handle it better because you are living from a position of strength. This strength comes from your soul and it is eternal, abundant and always available for you to tap into. You understand that this soul is the same universal soul that is available for all of us to share and prosper. You feel lighter and your presence will be an inspiration for others to connect with. People will notice you; they appreciate your presence and see the love in your eyes. Warm glow emanates from your body and through your spoken words, your actions are warm and gracious.

All the steps that we have covered thus far has transformed you to a warm and gracious being. You always had this inside of you, but for various reasons it was hidden. Now you are awakened. You are aware of all that is around you, both what you see with your eyes open and closed. You understand that you can have experiences that can not be explained by your physical senses. For example, you are thinking of accepting a new job across country and relocating to a new city and for a few days you keep seeing this new place advertised in the media. You are thinking of taking a vacation and a few days later you receive a special invitation in the mail to a new exotic place at a great price. You are worried about how you will be able to pay your bills next month as you just lost your job, and out of the blue, you get a residual check for a television commercial you did three years ago. These are experiences about coincidences, synchronicities or opportunities that come our way because we are living a warm and gracious life. We all have these experiences, some more than others, and this depends how connected you are with your creative optimum self. Living a warm and gracious life aligns you with the universal soul and the flow of life.

When you are warm and gracious, you have compassion, you are hospitable, approachable, genuine, and real. You are love. People and all creatures of life want to be connected with you because they see truth in you. They see a god in you and they are inspired. Sometimes, they will not express this because they do not think that they can be the same and they may feel intimidated. But over time, as you open up and connect with their soul, they will be inspired and realize that they also have the ability to be graceful, kind and a lover of life.

With this love, you are able to diffuse conflicts and bring harmony to a tense situation, whether or not you are there from the beginning. If arguments arise between two people before you arrive to the scene, they will pick up your warm and positive energy when you do arrive and will serve as an immediate relief. They know that you are there to assist and resolve the matter and that you have good intentions. The love you carry in your eyes and through your actions melts away the negativity that existed between the adversaries and guides them to connect with their inner wisdom and reach a compromise. If disagreements or difference of opinions arise while you are present, your wisdom and knowledge will quickly intervene and guide them to see the truth. Your energy will guide them to be reasonable and civil. If discussions take place after you leave, they will still feel your presence and will inspire them to work out a reasonable solution. This is transformation at its best. When you can bring light into a dark situation, whether or not they realize it was you. As a consultant, I observed and work through many situations like these. The most important tool that you can have to succeed is your self. If you live warm and gracious, you transform the moment that you are living into something magical and memorable.

As you share your love and grace with the world, you will connect with people who also live and share the same way. You are drawn to the same energy and when a group of people are bonded by this love and grace, anything is possible. Great ideas always emerge from a pool of like minded individuals; obstacles are easily surmountable when faced with a community issue; two strangers meet for the first time and sparks fly. These examples are all around us and we all experience them. As more people have these experiences, we create more harmony in the world. Together we are evolving and inspiring others to transform the world to a place where love, respect and peace is the only way of life. As you live your life with warm and grace, you become one with the universe.

This unity gives you better understanding on the workings of life. You realize that you create the life you are living by the choices you make. When you are consciously aware of the choices you are making and the consequences of these choices, you will experience the end results of your energy. If you make choices that are based in love by bringing harmony to you and those around you and express what is reasonable at the moment, you are rewarded with opportunities to advance your life and those around you. You will feel safe, protected and guided by your inner wisdom. This wisdom is eternal and has evolved over time and it is the same wisdom that lives in all of us.

It is the wisdom of the universe and it lives in the moment. Some people are not aware of this wisdom because they are temporarily disconnected while some others are connected but use it to make choices that solely better their lives while knowing that others will suffer as a result. They may feel that they have succeeded in getting what they want, but it will eventually catch up to them. The bad energy that they have created will return to them in some way, shape or form. It may take a while, perhaps another lifetime, but the universal soul is governed by truth and order. And like the saying goes, "what goes around, comes around." But if you live with grace, and you make choices that inadvertently cause pains and sufferings to others, the universe will correct itself by relieving that suffering in some way. When you are living with warm and grace, the universe protects you and all of us because we are all part of the same soul, the same COS. Together we can transform the world.

Step 8 Recap: Be Warm and Gracious

As you practice and live by the steps discussed so far, you have evolved into a warm and gracious being. You are more compassionate and understanding with your self and with people around you and an inspiration for others to be the same.

1. Live a warm and gracious life in all that you say and do and you will bring peace and harmony to each situation. You are awakened to a life of coincidences, synchronicities and opportunities. As you give your soul to the world, the universe will reveal to you all its gifts.

2. You diffuse conflicts, diminish anxieties and worries from all lives. You live a life from a position of strength and inspire others to do the same.

3. You are compassionate, genuine and approachable. You bond with all people and creatures of life and they want to be connected with you because they see truth in you. You bring out the very best in people and situations.

4. You are connected to your inner wisdom and it guides you to make conscious choices that brings peace, love and harmony to you and the world around you. You are in the flow of life and inspire others to live from their creative optimum self.

Exercise

This is a visual exercise and it will take 10-15 minutes. Find a comfortable place to sit quietly and alone. Close your eyes focus on your breathing and prepare yourself as if you were going to meditate. When you have reached a still place in your mind, imagine that you are sitting in a warm and cozy movie theatre. The theatre is almost full and there is big anticipation for this movie to begin. Everyone is thrilled to be watching this movie. It is premier night. Now select a movie that you love with an actor and character that you and everyone in the audience will love. Some ideas might be a James Bond movie, or an old classic with a dashing Jimmy Stewart, or a Katherine Hepburn. It can be movie that has a character that you would love to play if you were an actor yourself. This actor is a movie star and is loved by all. As you and everyone else watches this movie, observe how the movie star performs, notice the mannerism, how they speak, move, react, and their face expressions. Observe how it makes you feel elated and overjoyed by the movie and the performance of the movie star.

Now, imagine that you are able to move and sit right in front of the screen but facing the audience that is watching the movie. They can not see you but you can see them. Observe the joy they express in their eyes and how much fun they are having watching the movie star in this movie. Now, imagine that you magically become the star in the movie. See yourself in the movie playing the role of the star. See yourself in this character and emulate the way your movie star talks or you can talk the way you talk in real life. Just be the star in the movie and see how everyone loves your performance. The movie now ends and everyone applauds. Everyone is thrilled and inspired by your performance. The audience walks out of the theatre smiling, laughing and overjoyed by the experience.

This exercise is a reminder that life is like a movie. We are all stars in our movie, our story and we have an audience. We all have an opportunity to live our lives in a warm and gracious way that brings joy to our lives and to those around us. If you live with this passion, you inspire others to be movie stars as well.

Be passionate and grateful and life will reveal all its beauty.

STEP 9: **BE PASSIONATE AND GRATEFUL**

As you begin to live your life with warmth and grace you become passionate and grateful for your life. You have a zest for life and bring a magnetic force into every moment. Even when initially things do not work out the way you want them to, you learn to understand that sometimes we do not know all the hidden details and in the long run this may not be the wisest decision for you. You feel safe and protected that life and the universe is on your side even in the middle of despair. If you are not connected with your creative optimum self, you will more readily fall into the trap of feeling sorry for yourself or feeling depressed about life. These are real emotions at the human level, but if you observe these emotions from the soul level, or as you remain connected to your COS, you gain a better understanding of the situation and gain more wisdom in life as a result.

In every experience in life, there is a lesson to be learned. When my father unexpectedly died at the age of 57, it was a very low point in my life. I was very close with my father even though I did not agree with how he handled things at times. Still, I appreciate the goodness that existed within him.

When he fell into a coma, it was devastating for my family. The doctors informed us that he will most likely remain in this state for the rest of his life, he was brain dead. We had to make a decision whether to keep him in this state or choose to remove him from the respirator. He had no living will so the decision was left to us. Initially, it was a difficult decision for us to make, but as my father remained in a coma for ten days the decision came easier. His body did not move, he just had tears in his eyes. Those tears spoke to me - he was sad to be leaving this life but knew that it would be the right thing for all of us. Over time, I came to terms with his death and learned to appreciate life even more and to live a passionate life with no regrets. My father had regrets before he died, for not being able to change and do some things differently. He had lost his connection to his inner wisdom and passion for life.

Here's another example – I was working on Wall Street for a major bank, a senior position making $150,000/yr. living on Park Avenue in New York City. I was thirty years old and a bachelor. I enjoyed traveling every few months on business to Europe and took regular vacations to exotic places. Everyone thought I had a great life, and so did I. After a while, I realized that my work was consuming me and I was not happy. I loved the type of work but was not appreciated for what I produced. People would knock down my ideas in one moment and later learned that they had used the same ideas to advance their career. I was not happy anymore and I realized that it was impacting my personal life as well. I was going out every night, staying up late and not taking care of myself. My stress level escalated so much that at work I would regularly have my blood pressure checked and it had skyrocketed to 170/110. The low point arrived one night after having dinner with my girlfriend. Out of the blue, she proposed and offered

me a ring. We never had discussed this. Even though it was
a sweet gesture, I was not ready for this. This added to my
stress and on top of this, I and ten other people were struck
with food poisoning that night. When it rains it pours! Well,
that night I broke down. I ended it up at the hospital to be
treated for food poisoning but I know that the accumulated
stress had a lot to do with it. When I returned home, I was
up all night crying. I was depressed and I remember hearing
a voice inside of me saying, "find me", and I did. I left my
job, New York City, and returned to my family home. There,
I picked up journaling again. Through my writing, I learned
that I was not living a passionate life. I was not happy with
my job, it was not creative enough. I was raised by a mother
who was very creative and had so much zest for life, even during the difficult times. I had lost that passion and I allowed
stress to block me from being truthful with myself. That was a
big turning point for me and it later fueled me to expand my
transformation work into my consulting practice.

By staying connected with your creative optimum self,
you will live a life of passion and you will bring this passion
to all the work that you do. Some people choose to remain in
the same career such as a doctor, law enforcement, teacher, actor, farmer or thousands of other professions. Others change
careers a couple of times or follow a career that allows them
to work in many industries. It can be anything that you wish
as long as you have the enthusiasm and enjoy the work. You
need to be truthful with your self in what you want to do;
if you are not happy with your work your body and mind
will complain. It may take some time but it will happen.
Choose the kind of work that fuels your interests, that makes
you want to do cartwheels and you feel exhilarated. You can
change career along the way but always work with passion as
it will align you with the flow of life. In this flow, you allow

life to take you on this journey of discovery.

While on this journey, you know that this moment is the only thing that is important and if you focus on the moment, you can create the life you want. You enjoy anything that you do, even daily chores, because you know that the harmonious energy you are giving while cooking for example, is creating a delicious meal for you and your family to enjoy. Everything comes out perfectly when you have passion, nothing can stop you. As you live a passionate life you learn to appreciate and give gratitude to all that you have. You understand that as you share this wonderful meal, there are people in the world who are not able to share any kind of meal with loved ones, or have no food at all. When you are grateful with what you have and acknowledge that you are living a blessed life, you are aligned with the universal love. Be thankful of the air that you breathe, the flowers you see and the stars up in the sky. You are giving good karma to the universe and you will inspire others to do the same.

Living a life of gratitude alerts the universal soul that you are ready for more blessings to come into your life. Opportunities will find you and fall into your lap because you are in the flow of life. Sometimes these opportunities are out of the blue and you would have never thought of them, but they may be very prosperous for you and the universe at large. The universe has trust in you and will offer you new chances because it has faith and knows that you are ready for something new. The universe needs you just as much as you need it. Learn from the universe and the passion it has for allowing life on earth to prosper over time. We do not worry or make the earth go around at the speed of light in space. It just happens, the universe allows this. We trust the universe to perform this and millions of other creations and tasks.

The universe is passionate about the work that it does and we can be the same. Live a passionate and grateful life and the universe will bless you with zest and more creativity. As more people live a passionate and grateful life, the world will transform into a place where peace, love and harmony is available at all times.

Step 9 Recap: Be Passionate and Grateful

Living a passionate and grateful life will make you a lover of life and you will bring this abundance into each moment of your life.

1. By living your life with passion, you follow the flow of life and do and say everything perfectly. You follow where life takes you, and appreciate each experience and live with no regrets. You gain knowledge and wisdom from each experience.
2. You feel safe and protected in life and you know that the universe is on your side. You trust that when things do not go as planned that there is something to be learned and something better to do in life. With patience and insight, you understand the path to follow that brings harmony to you and those around you.
3. Be thankful and appreciate all that you have in life. Show your enthusiasm in everything you do and say and appreciate all of your experiences. The universe is grateful and will send more opportunities your way. The universe has faith and trust in you and your creative optimum self.

Exercise

There are two parts to this exercise. In the first part, make a list in your journal of all the passions in your life. For example, some of my current passions in life are I love performances in the arts, love cooking for friends, running on the beach, solving complex problems, guiding others to find their creative optimum self and transforming the world. Make a list of ten items that you are passionate about. For each of your passions, give an action item on what you can do to carry out your passion. For example, on my list, I love to cook for friends, so I will invite my friends over one night for a delicious meal. I am passionate about guiding others to connect with their creative optimum self, so I am going to write a book. Make sure that you pick action items that are practical and you intent to follow through, otherwise you will have a loose end. For each action item, give a due date and include it in your plan of things that you will do. If you track progress and carry out your action items, you will gain more passion for life because you will feel good that you are doing something that you love. And others will be inspired to follow their passion.

For the second exercise, write in your journal all the things in your life that you are thankful for. It can be your home, family, job, the air that you breathe, the way the sun shines on the window. It could be anything and everything that you feel that you are blessed with. And you can make the list as long as you want. Once you complete the list, keep this list in your daily journal or somewhere handy so that you can revisit when you meditate. As you meditate daily, be aware of all the things you are thankful for. Either visualize the gratitude you have in your life or write them in more detail in your journal. As you take time to give thanks to what you have, you are aligned with the universal flow and your creative optimum self. You are open to receive more from the universe and inspire others to give thanks for all the blessings in their lives. As more people live with passion and give thanks to all the wonderful things in their lives, the world will transform into a place of blessed harmony. We become the eyes and ears of the universe.

*Live from your Creative Optimum Self and
all the secrets of life will be revealed to you.*

STEP 10: **LIVE FROM YOUR COS - EYES AND EARS OF THE UNIVERSE**

As you live a passionate and grateful life and incorporate the *inner* and *outer* steps into your daily life, you are living from your soul. You are connected with this inner guide, your creative optimum self and you have transformed your life. How is your life transformed? You feel lighter, safer in life, with less worry, and know that you are part of something special as you bond with the universe. You see beauty in all things, plants, flowers, people, animals, the sky and the oceans. You find inspiration in all these things. You are awakened to a world you never thought existed. You find it easier to smile, laugh and bring this same joy to other people. You are concerned about all of life and not just your family and friends, but even strangers. You support, guide and protect the less fortunate. You are truthful and ensure that others follow the same truth. You are fearless like a spiritual warrior dedicated to ensure that knowledge and wisdom exists in each moment. You are elegant, refined and civil and you stand up for what is right. You have more clarity and you are more aware of things and see and hear things that others may not. You are the eyes and ears of the universe.

Over time, you will see and hear things you never did before. You will see beyond what is capable by your eyes – whether open or closed. You will see light in the sun and in the shadows; love in good people and in "evil" people. You will see what the universe sees, and as you see more, the universe will further reveal itself. You will see opportunities when everyone else sees failures, a solution when everyone sees a problem. You will see years ahead when everyone sees the past. You will see a world of peace, love and harmony and all the possibilities that exist. You will see the synchronicities and connections of all things, and you will see yourself doing things that you never thought would be possible. You will see a new world: no racism, violence, hatred, discrimination, and injustice; a world of peace and love. People will be drawn to you. Your aura and openness will melt away any differences. You have a magnetism that they wish in themselves and they want to share time with you. And when they do, they will be inspired to be the same. They will see your grace, love and harmony. They will begin to see your vision, new world and will be inspired to live from their COS as well.

As you continue to live from your soul, you become more aware of sights, sounds and voices around you and you hear the universe speak to you. The universe speaks through your relationships and strangers you meet on the street. The universe guides you on to the right path. If you are thinking about a problem and you need guidance on how to solve it, you may get the answer from the sea as you walk on the beach, from a character as you watch a movie or from a stranger as you walk down the street. If you are considering taking on a new job, you will hear news about this company from the TV, radio or the subway chatter. This news will assist you in making the right decision about whether to take the new job. If you are considering a move to a new city and you wish you knew a realtor that can help you find a place, you meet someone who knows a realtor or you connect with the right one as you go through the online directory. If you are not feeling well and think you should visit the doctor, you then get a call from your doctor that you are due for the annual physical. You are thinking of a friend, the phone rings and it is your friend. As you stay connected with your soul, you will be more aware of these experiences and synchronicities that occur on a daily basis. Your soul is aligned with the universal soul and you have this bond, a special relationship. You ask and you receive. As you give love and harmony to the world, the universe receives this warm energy and keeps things flowing. You are co-creating your life and that of the world by staying connected with your soul.

Living from your soul gives you abundant energy to live an optimal life. You have more energy, focus and precision to carry out each moment of your life in the best way possible. You are focus at your work, when you cook, talk, walk and even when you sleep. You sleep more comfortably, have more clarity in your dreams and have a better understanding of your dreams and the connections to the waking life. You excel at anything that you do because you are living in the moment and this moment has all the wisdom and knowledge that you need. As you practice living from the present, you have experiences that can not be explained by the rational mind. You feel a deep connection with people because you are part of the same universal soul. You are placed in a same situation with someone you connect with and both come up with the same idea or finish the same sentence or have a feeling of déjà vu. You are both in the moment and have access to the same wisdom that exists in that moment. You are making love with your lover and you feel a sensation that is beyond physical, you transcend to a place where it is silent and yet filled with ecstasy and bliss. This place is the moment and has all the energy you need to beautifully carry out the experience you wish to share. You are sitting watching the sunset and you are inspired to write a poem about the beauty of the sunset. Then, a year later you pick up a book of poems and there is a poem very similar to yours with a picture of a sunset. At the time that you were connected with the sunset and your soul, there was someone else experiencing a similar moment and received the same inspiration as you did.

The same goes with your intentions. You write in your journal a creative idea for a book or a business plan for a product or a lyric for a song. If you meditate on these thoughts and visualize carrying out the intentions, when the time is right, they will transform into reality. Your intentions are messages to the universe and by staying connected with your COS, the intentions will one day become a reality. As more creativity is fused into the world, the world will function at a more optimal level and transformation to a world of peace, love and harmony will naturally occur.

As you continue to live from your soul with eyes and ears of the universe you have transformed yourself into a higher being. Your body that houses this soulful being is lighter, with more energy and blissfully happy. Why? Because you are in the moment and enjoying life to the fullest. You are unafraid of death because you understand that life and death are part of this journey. While the body may die one day, the wisdom that lives in the moment today and that you experience and connect to, will always remain here. And so will your soul. Remember, in this moment, earth is spinning at the speed of light. It is so fast that our eyes can not see it go so fast. But we are and we are able to function just fine. We can walk a straight line and we do not see ourselves tumbling around in a ball. But we are, at a deep level. There are things that we can not physically see. One of these is that we are made of the same stuff. We are all made of energy that swirls together like a beautiful dance and most of this is made up of empty space. The energy is so small that it does not even register in the physical world. At this level, life takes on a new meaning. The physical life that we experience is a small part of the bigger life that exists. And the bigger life is that we all share the same energy, we interconnect, overlap and we are locked in. Next time that you experience moments that are magical and breathtaking, out of the ordinary, witness a miracle or a connection that is simply out of this world, realize that you are living The Way. You are transforming while dancing with the universe. Honor and respect these experiences and treat them kindly. As more people live The Way, the world will transform while the stars in the universe continue to dance into eternity.

Step 10 Recap: Live from Your COS - Eyes and Ears of the Universe

As you reach step ten, you realize that you are living from the soul and you have become the eyes and ears of the universe.

1. Living from your soul bonds you with your creative optimum self. You live in a world of peace, love and harmony. You find beauty in all people and all things.
2. You connect with all people, creatures and all of things, seen and unseen. You gain access to all the wisdom and knowledge that exists in each moment. You have no fears and no worries. Not even of death because you realize that

your soul will never die.

3. You realize that you are one with the universe and that we are all connected and come from the same universal soul. You realize that you have transformed into a loving being and nothing will give you greater joy than to see the world transform into a more loving place. By living from your soul, you will inspire others to be the same and the world will indeed transform.

Exercise

This is a visual exercise. Prepare yourself as if you were going to meditate. Once you have found a quiet place in your mind, where you have no thoughts, simply focus on your breath. Now imagine that you are the lens of a video camera. Imagine that you are filming yourself where you are in this moment with this lens. If you are sitting on a bed facing the window, imagine that you, the lens, is facing opposite of your body and focusing on your body. The image in your mind should be you sitting there on the bed. You, as the lens, can see your eyes, nose, the bed, the room, all the details of your body and the room. Continue to imagine the rest of your home through your lens, go to the kitchen, the bedroom, the bathroom, and all its furniture. Be as detail as possible and give it your full attention. Now, move your lens out of your home and film the details of the building, and all the faces of the residences and workers. See all these images through your lens in your mind. Now imagine, taking your lens outside into the street and see the faces of all the people on the streets, the place of your work, your colleagues, and the rest of the city. Through your lens, film the parks and all the places you

visit and let these images appear in your mind. Now, visit
your friends, family, all of your relationships, nature, the
country you live in and places you have visited in the past. Let
you lens zoom around the world and pick up all images you
see. Continue soaring around the world, through your lens,
capture all the images you see until you reach the stars. See
all these images in your mind and as you imagine this, give it
your full attention. Focus on the images and give it your love.
Stay with these images for a few more minutes and when you
are ready, take your time to open your eyes.

Practice this exercise each time you meditate. Let this be
the last part of your meditation. Over time and with practice,
you will see yourself as the eyes and ears of the universe. You
are love and as you give your attention to all of the moments
in your life, you will give love and harmony to everyone and
to everything that you do. You will melt away disputes, by
visualizing in advance peace rather than conflicts, you will
resolve a problem by seeing a solution, you will heal the sick,
by sending warm and good wishes. As you give love to everything you do and places you go, you will transform it into a
love thing and a loving place. You will inspire others to transform and together the world will be transformed into a more
peaceful, harmonious and loving place - heaven on earth. This
is The Way.

Transforming the world takes you to heaven on earth.

CONCLUSION

TRANSFORMING THE WORLD - NEVER ENDING JOURNEY

As you practice and live with the ten *inner* and *outer* steps you will learn to stay connected with your inner wisdom. This inner wisdom is your creative optimum self and as you live from this self, you are living The Way. Living The Way connects you to the universal soul and allows you to live a life of peace, harmony and love. And as you continue on this journey, you will inspire others to live the same. And as more people practice and live with these steps, we will transform the world. This transformation is not a dream. It is a reality and a wonderful never ending journey.

The ten steps described here are simple and practical, and not a secret! I invite you to execute them by incorporating them into your daily life and observe for yourself the positive changes in your life. Some people will take longer than others and it is important that we support one another along the way. This is a journey with no end date – the more you practice living from your soul, the more you will learn. Over time you will gain more knowledge and wisdom and will continue to do so as long as you stay on this journey. Don't be hard on yourself if you think things are not moving as quickly. They probably are, you may not be aware of it in the beginning but you will over time. This is a personal journey, with no competition or prize whoever finishes first. This is a journey that evolves and will continue as long as you live through your creative optimum self.

The steps are evolutionary – they will move you from one step to the next as you tap into your COS. And it all begins by picking up a pen and journaling. Keep your writing simple, begin writing down how are you feeling at the moment and over time, the source of creativity will open up. But first, you need to peel away the layers of social conditioning that has accumulated over time. You peel away by writing the anxieties, fears, worries, pains, disappointments you have piled up over the years. And as you do this, you will quiet down the chatter and meet your inner guide. This inner guide is always available to you and as you begin to meditate on a regular basis, you learn to gain access to this wisdom. Meditation helps you to understand that there is another layer or existence in your life that is beyond the physical world. You will transcend to a quiet, soulful place, a field of all possibilities. To stay connected to your soul, you need to protect yourself from all the distractions of life and you can do this by reading inspirational material regularly. Nurture your mind and soul with essays, poems, stories that stir your emotions, expand your horizons and stimulate your intelligence. Be curious about new things and read stories that inspire and teach you something about life. As you continue on this journey, you will notice that you enjoy spending time with nature and in solitude as it gives you great comfort and peace. You learn from nature how to live harmoniously, gracefully and compassionately. You learn to appreciate the connection between your body and soul. Your soul is housed in your body, and you realize that your overall well being is important to the health of your body and soul. When your body is at its optimal self, then the body allows the soul to live through beautifully. You begin to listen to your body and it will inform you the type and amount of food it needs, how much sleep, the type of exercises, and when the body needs special care. By nurturing your body, you will have less stress and anxiety and your life is becoming more optimal.

As you progress on this path, you will begin to live with no loose ends. You realize that following through with your positive intentions and actions keeps you lighter with no clutter in your mind and environment. You have more energy and you are moving with the flow of life. You are becoming more compassionate and understanding of people and you realize that you can learn so much about yourself and life by nurturing all of your relationships. As you respect, love and are honest with your self, family, friends, community, col-leagues, all the people you meet on a daily basis, and nature, you realize that we are all connected. We may look differently, but we are part of the same universal soul. As we learn to be more compassionate, kind and truthful in our relationships, we become more warm and gracious and we share this love with the world. This love diffuses conflicts, brings harmony and inspires others to do the same. You have an abundant of wonderful energy and you become passionate in anything that you do. And anything you do is magical. You are grateful for all that you have. You consume less energy and you fuel your moments with creativity and inspiration. As you continue your passionate life, you become more aware of your self and the universe. You feel the soul with you at all times and feel the universe flowing through you - you have become the eyes and ears of the universe. As you live your life from your soul, you have more clarity in what you see and hear. You feel safe and trust life where it takes you because you know that the universe is on your side. You create the life you want and your life is magical. You have transformed your life into peace, love and harmony and as you continue to transform, you will inspire and guide others to connect with their creative optimum self. As we all continue on this journey, we will transform our lives, and the world will transform into a more compassionate, peaceful and harmonious place.

There you have it – The Way. Transforming the world through your creative optimum self is not a dream but a possibility. Each one of us has a responsibility and the free will to do its part. And you can do this by following the *inner* and *outer* steps described here. The COS steps are simple and practical and they do not cost anything. They are free and available to all. If you do your part, stay organized and follow your journey, you will inspire others to do the same. And if we all continue on this journey, we will have a transformed world. I thank you in advance for making this world a better place for all of us to enjoy.

ABOUT THE AUTHOR

Costantino Delli is passionate about business, personal and global transformation. He founded COS International in 1995 after an accelerated, seven year corporate executive career, starting with Wachovia Securities, Science Applications International Corp, Bloomberg Financial Markets and Bankers Trust. Through his work, he has delivered Creative Optimum Solutions for transforming and advancing Fortune 100 companies, small businesses and organizations. Clients have reaped the benefits in terms of increase in productivity, cost savings and additional revenue.

Tapping into the arts, science, personal experiences and business success, he has developed "The Way", a practical guide for people from all walks of life to reconnect to their Creative Optimum Self and transform their lives. He wishes to share the *inner* and *outer* steps with the rest of you to inspire and empower you to live your greatest life. Through his own experiences and observations in life, he recognizes the power that each of us have to create a better world for everyone. Together, we can have a world where peace, love and harmony are the only way of life.

Ten percent of the proceeds from this book will go to the COS Foundation. This foundation supports children and adult programs that educate and guide all to incorporate these steps into their lives. Costantino knows that if we can share, leverage and support our efforts, we can achieve more, become greater and inspire the rest. And together, we can transform the world.

Costantino was born and raised in Taranto, Italy, a beautiful and ancient Southern City on the Ionian Coast. At the age of eight his parents decided to move his family to the U.S. and settled in Trenton N.J. A graduate with honors from Rutgers University majoring in mathematics, Costantino has traveled the world and calls "home" wherever he is at the moment. He currently makes his home in beautiful, sunny California with his wife Tanya and precious Merlin, their Russian Blue.

Please visit www.cosinternational.org for additional information about the author.